ANTAGONISTS ADVOCATES and ALLIES

THE WAKE UP CALL GUIDE
FOR WHITE WOMEN
WHO WANT TO BECOME ALLIES
WITH BLACK WOMEN

CATRICE M. JACKSON
INTERNATIONAL BEST-SELLING AUTHOR

Catriceology
Show Up, Shine & Do The Damn Thing

Published by Catriceology Enterprises,
LLC Omaha, NE | United States of America
Copyright © 2015-2019 by Catrice M. Jackson

The author has made every effort to ensure the accuracy of the information within this book was correct at the time of publication. The author does not assume and hereby disclaims any liability to any party for any loss, damage, or disruption caused by errors or omissions, whether such errors or omissions result from accident, negligence, or any other cause.

FOR INFORMATION CONTACT: Catrice M. Jackson, M.S., LMHP, LPC, Global Visionary Leader of the Awakened Conscious Shift, Racial Justice Educator, Speaker, and International Best-Selling Author.

Online ordering is available for all products.
www.amazon.com

WEBSITES
www.catriceology.com
www.shetalkswetalk.com
www.catriceologyenterprises.com

ISBN-13: 978-0983839828
ISBN-10: 0983839824

Book Cover Design: Kerri Liu
Editor: Marian Gallagher
Interior Design: Kerri Liu

Printed in the USA 10 9 8 7 6 5 4 3 2

ANTAGONiSTS
ADVOCATES
and ALLiES

THE WAKE UP CALL GUIDE

FOR WHITE WOMEN

WHO WANT TO BECOME ALLIES

WITH BLACK WOMEN

ENDORSEMENTS

"The division within feminism is caused by White women. In particular, by our denial of White Privilege, and when we use our White Privilege to take refuge from the fight against racism. *Antagonists, Advocates, and Allies* states the problem (Denial of White Privilege), and clears the way for White women to 'get off the fence and walk their talk.' If we White women can do so, then long-standing relationships, friendships, and warriorships can be forged with Black women and Women of Color. They are wondering where we are and what's taking us so long to show up. After reading this book, you will wonder that yourself. White women have a lot of work to do. And we need to move fast. Catrice's book will inspire you to consciously quicken your pace. I'm grateful Catrice wrote this book. I only wish she didn't have to. One thing I know for certain is that once you have read her words, you will be grateful she wrote it too. It's time we, as White women, wake up and do better."

—*Alex Clarke, Author and Playwright*

"The issues of racial discord and White Privilege are thorny ones. Catrice M. Jackson is boldly addressing the problem head on, with blunt talk meant to shake White women out of their complacency and into greater awareness of our part in our collective cultural dysfunction. This is a powerful treatise on race and White female power specifically, and thus it is needfully, deliberately provocative. This is good. Catrice is to be commended for bringing this conversation forward and initiating a tough talk that absolutely needs to be had. Listen up; the disenfranchised are speaking directly and eloquently. And while you, my fellow White women, might find some of what she says confrontational or perhaps too strident for your tastes, bear in mind that it's your filters that are the challenge, not her words. Be quiet, and listen. Read this."

—*Molly Burke, CPCC, MSU, Queen of Confidence and*
Type B Whisperer, Trainer, Author, Speaker

"If you have spent any time on social media in the last several years, you may be aware of words and phrases like 'White Privilege,' 'Microaggressions,' and 'Intersectionality.' Even if you know what they mean—but especially if you don't—this book offers a crucial, direct breakdown of why it is increasingly important that White women understand how they impact Black women, and why we should care. There's no mincing of words here: It is tough love for White women, an urgent call to recognize that any women's movement that ignores, sidelines, and denies the experiences of Black women is no movement at all. White women should read this book because it is a straightforward assessment of the way we too often minimize, erase, ignore, or willfully deny the experiences of Black women. This book anticipates our excuses and rationalizations and firmly rejects them. Catrice provides tools for White women to understand why women's movements must be intersectional if we are going to affect change in an unequal world."

—*Andi Zeisler, Editorial/Creative Director, Bitch Media*

"Every person, regardless of race, who is committed to making their community a better place needs to read this book. Make no mistake, Catrice M. Jackson has no interest whatsoever in providing you with a flowery, rose-colored message. She is committed to shaking you out of your complacent existence and into a real and frank conversation about the escalating racial tension in our country, and how we can learn from one another, educate ourselves, overcome and improve. The reading is not comfortable, and it may make you wince or disagree, but I will guarantee this: the message is sincere. *Antagonists, Advocates, and Allies* will change everything you know about the phrase 'what if.' Buckle up for one hell of a ride! You will never be the same after reading this!"

—*Angela Sulkowski, Accountant, Mother, and
Fellow Game Changer*

"What now comes to the surface in forceful ways are the deep wounds still remaining to heal, in particular racial injustice, whether overt or silent. Despicable, unbearable acts are increasing and becoming more and more visible and can no longer be ignored. A new, authentic dialogue is necessary to initiate change, and White women need to find their place and know whether they are actors of change or contributors to the ills of our society. In *Antagonists, Advocates, and Allies*, Catrice M. Jackson unapologetically sheds light on the dark spots of our privileges of being White in America today, and helps us (White women) really look at where we are and decide for ourselves whether we are truly authentic when we speak about all women in America. She challenges us to examine our feminism to hopefully make a change to really become Allies. When we truly feel and hear the pain that another human being shares without defending ourselves behind excuses, then maybe we will know true compassion and become closer to the Divine Feminine change we are meant to bring."

—*Sabrina Mizerek, Owner of Mindful Home and Body, LLC*

"Catrice has seriously delivered some hard-hitting, powerful, and truthful insights in *Antagonists, Advocates, and Allies*. Get ready to have your world rocked! She is unapologetic in her delivery and her message. I found the book to be deep, beautiful, and incredibly honest. Buckle up; you're in for a hell of a ride on this journey with Catrice. It's awesome and you'll arrive on the other side feeling like you took a big ole deep breath of fresh air, pure and raw."

—Dortha Hise, Chief Overwhelm Eliminator, Pretty Smart *Virtual Services*

"*Antagonists, Advocates, and Allies* is EPIC and thought-provoking! This book is not only about how to be an Ally to our Black soul sisters, but it goes so much further and deeper beyond that. It's a message that reminds us to be an Ally to all our kindred soul sisters; to truly seek to understand someone's truths, especially when they are not aligned with your own. Because at the depths of that exploration is where true growth and expansion happens for all parties involved. Catrice is a woman on a God-sent mission, looking for her Allies who've come with the same mission: to create a soul tribal council, create conscious shifts, and facilitate growth and breakthroughs beyond anything else we've ever experienced before!"

—*Morgan Field, Epic Sexy YOU, Certified Life Coach, The Ultimate Code Breaker, and Speaker*

"Forget the glass ceiling, there is a glass wall between White women and women of color, and Catrice has shattered it with this book. The glass ceiling and other overtly oppressive injustices promoted in social media today have allowed a more covert and sinister injustice to go unnoticed and unaddressed—until now. I've often felt this invisible barrier between myself and my White women friends that until now I could not put my finger on. This is a painful yet cathartic read. In *Antagonists, Advocates, and Allies*, Catrice is both loving and firm as she calls White women to drop the pretenses and lays out a blueprint for how ALL women can honor each other with compassion and truly join together to change the world. White women should read this book if they want to foster real meaningful relationships with women of color and to truly be effective in the fight for women's rights and racial equality. And because willful or unintentional ignorance on this issue fans the flames of racial and gender bias that breeds the very violence and hate many profess to fight. True collaboration and women's empowerment can happen only when they are inclusive of women of all colors and experiences."

—*Kenya Halliburton, Online Business Mastery Expert*

"Catrice Jackson's thorough analysis of the precarious relationship between Black and White women is breathtaking and refreshing! The main reason I felt the need to create a business networking organization for Black women is because when I would stumble upon female entrepreneurial organizations on the Internet that appeared to have been created for ALL women, I was hard-pressed to locate women on these organization's websites who were women of color. In *Antagonists, Advocates, and Allies*, Catrice has managed to thrust into the spotlight and onto the stage the feelings Black women have held for years, but dared not speak! Bravo, bravo, bravo!"

—*Carmin Wharton, Founder, e-BlackWomenNetwork*

"In 1963, Betty Friedan wrote the book *The Feminist Mystique*, in which she discussed 'a problem with no name' experienced by middle-class suburban White women. The 'problem with no name' was grounded in the White woman's role as defined by her White male counterpart; the idea that they should be happy living in their feminine roles of wives, mothers, and homemakers, etc. Well, in 2015, the Post-World War II, White middle-class female 'problem with no name' survived and has been transformed into a name: 'Privilege.' In *Antagonists, Advocates, and Allies*, Catrice M. Jackson uses an in-your-face approach to unearth the cognitive dissonance of White women in their relationships or lack thereof with women of color, in particular Black women in the Women's Empowerment arena. If women dare to read this book, they will experience a catharsis! It's witty, informative, and refreshing."

—*Lawanda Brown, Academic Advisor and Sociology Adjunct*

DEDICATION

For Tahsahn and Tyson

The greatest gift I ever received was a man child who came through me as a gift from God. My son, my breath, shaped and transformed my life in ways that nothing else ever has. God gave me my son at a time in my life when I needed him most. My son chose me at a time when I needed to know how to love and needed to be loved unconditionally. I never knew real love until I looked into his beautiful big brown eyes for the very first time. THIS was love at first sight. My son gave my life meaning, depth, purpose, and direction.

He's been my greatest joy, my most profitable investment, and raising him from a boy to a man has been my greatest accomplishment. He's been my greatest teacher, and I've learned more about life, love, and purpose because of his presence than from any other experience. If I'm never called by any other name, being called "Mother" has been enough. Son, I hope you dedicate your life to God and his purpose for your life. Always be faithful, and never ever give up on your dreams. You are a child of the most high KING and you too are a king. The greatest role you can embody is father. Be the best father you can be, and make sure your kings and queens know they are children of the one and only God. There is nothing you and your children can't have. *"Ask, and it will be given to you; seek, and you will find; knock, and it will be opened to you"* (Matt. 7:7).

This book, this message, my truth is written for my son, my only child, my seed, and my legacy. Lauryn Hill's song "To Zion" tells our story perfectly. I love you, Son, more than my own breath. Thank you for choosing and loving me. Always remember: *"I can do all things through Christ who strengthens me" (Phil. 4:13).*

TO ZION

Unsure of what the balance held
I touched my belly overwhelmed
By what I had been chosen to perform
But then an angel came one day
Told me to kneel down and pray
For unto me a man child would be born
Woe this crazy circumstance
I knew his life deserved a chance
But everybody told me to be smart
Look at your career they said
Lauryn, baby use your head
But instead I chose to use my heart

Now the joy of my world is in Zion
Now the joy of my world is in Zion

How beautiful if nothing more
Than to wait at Zion's door
I've never been in love like this before
Now let me pray to keep you from
The perils that will surely come
See life for you my prince has just begun

And I thank you for choosing me
To come through unto life to be
A beautiful reflection of his grace
For I know that a gift so great
Is only one God could create
And I'm reminded every time I see your face

—Lauryn Hill, Singer and Songwriter

I dedicate this book to my grandson Tyson. Until you experience it, you can't imagine you could ever love anyone more than your own children. When you are blessed with grandchildren, you know it's possible, and it's the ultimate joy to shower your grandchildren with the love you have for your own children. Tyson, you've brought so much joy, love, and happiness into our lives. You too are a divine gift from God, and I'm so grateful for your presence. You, my son, are a king and a child of God, which makes you an heir to his throne. You are here for a purpose, and I hope one day you discover it and boldly live out your special assignment in the world. Nana loves you. You'll always be my Sweetie Pie.

CATRICE M. JACKSON

TABLE OF CONTENTS

CATRICE M. JACKSON

PREFACE

I wrote this book because...

My life depends on it.

My soul refused to allow me to silence this message any longer.

I've been carrying the weight of this message all my life.

It's the truth.

I am not afraid... I was born for this. This is my message and my purpose.

I owe it to my mother and my grandmother, and to my great-grandmother, who was a slave.

Racism is a target on my son's back with every breath he takes.

Racism will be a target on my grandson's back if racism is not eliminated.

Nothing will change unless we stop white-washing and sugar-coating racism.

Too many Black and brown people are being killed because of racism and internalized oppression.

Too many women of color and Black women are suffering from racism in silence.

Too many White women are the oppressors of their suffering.

To set the souls of women of color and Black women free by speaking truth.

To provide affirmation and healing for my Black and brown sisters.

To encourage White women to step up and become Allies.

There are not enough White Allies to help eliminate the dis-ease called racism.

Too many White women are still in denial of their White Privilege and its collateral damage.

Racism begins and ends with you.

Too many women are being excluded and denied because of grown women acting like girls.

To eliminate Cliques, Catfights, and Colorblindness.

I believe it will be the unification of women that will break down the systems of oppression, transform the human condition, and cultivate world peace.

To empower women to first heal and save ourselves so that WE can heal and save the world!

"The truth will set you free, but first it will piss you off."

—Gloria Steinem

IF YOU WANT MEN TO ALIGN WITH WOMEN TO FIGHT GENDER INEQUALITY, THEN YOU MUST ALIGN WITH WOMEN OF COLOR TO FIGHT RACIAL INEQUALITY.

CATRICE M. JACKSON

INTRODUCTION

THIS IS YOUR WAKE-UP CALL!

Dear White Woman,

You have been privileged for far too long and have had your say when it comes to gender and race. Today is the day you sit down and listen without interrupting, projecting, minimizing, denying, blaming, justifying, or becoming offended and defensive. Your White Fragility pass has been revoked. It has expired and shall not be renewed.

You've had centuries of opportunities to express how you feel, say what you desire, and impose your privileged views, values, rules, guidelines, and experiences onto women of color and Black women, but today, my sister, you are not the teacher! Today you are a student, sitting in a class that will forever change your life, but only if you listen and finally hear what we have to say.

You've been talking, teaching, lecturing, leading, directing, and dominating the conversation around feminism, feminine power, and women's rights since you took your first breath. Now is the time that WE speak and you listen—and not just listen, but hear with your heart and soul. For centuries you have listened... but you have not truly heard our voices, our stories, our pain, our struggles, our experiences, our realities, and our truths.

You see... it's always been about you. The world has been laid at your feet on a silver platter. Men have adored you, protected you, and rescued you. Society has lifted you up, put you on a pedestal, and crowned you as the epitome of womanhood. Magazine covers have idolized you and made you iconic. Fashion designers have slated you as the ideal woman with the perfect body type. Department stores have crystallized your image into mannequins that some women envy and others despise.

Women around the world have envied you and have desired to be you, with everything you have. Meanwhile, you have knowingly and unknowingly dismissed, denied, and abused your power and privilege without realizing the magnitude of the collateral damage your unconsciousness has caused—the damage that only you can clean up to help restore social harmony among all women and swiftly usher in racial justice for women of color and Black women. The voice you are about to hear speaking to you through this book will not hesitate to be fully expressed, will not censor to soothe, and will not turn down the volume or lighten the tone to make you comfortable. You've been comfortable and coddled for far too long, and although you don't realize it yet, it's been to your detriment. Before you proceed to the first chapter of this book, you can easily determine whether you are an Antagonist, Advocate, or Ally. What I've expressed thus far will stir something up inside of you, something that will provide a clear indication of where you stand in relation to privilege, race, and racism:

- *If you are angry, pissed, offended, appalled, bewildered, in shock, livid, or hurt by my Dear White Woman letter, you are indeed an **Antagonist**.*

- *If you are in partial agreement with my letter, but it still offends you and you don't know what to do next, you just may be an **Advocate**.*

- *If you are saying, **"YES, Catrice, it's about time someone spoke these words,"** and you are standing up and challenging other White women on their privilege and racism, you are showing up like an **Ally**.*

You may be wondering why this book focuses on White and Black women. There are several reasons why. While I identify as a woman of color, my truths and my experiences are that of a Black woman; therefore, I can best speak on what is REAL for me and many Black women like me. But rest assured, and believe it or not, your White Privilege affects other women of color in similar ways. And to be quite honest, when I think about who has caused the most racial pain in my life, nine times out of ten, it has been a White woman.

You don't have to listen to me, and if you are indeed an Antagonist, you won't. You can close this book right now, head right on back to Privilegeville, go on with life as usual, and continue to Antagonize the very Black women you say you love, support, value, and empower. Or you can sit down, take a seat, listen, and hear this message deeply and profoundly.

Please take note:

- *I don't need or want your sympathy.*
- *I don't need you to apologize.*
- *I don't want you to feel sorry and helpless.*
- *I won't be accepting **any** of your statistics or textbook references related to race and racism. Don't bother sending them my way.*
- *I won't be considering any "isms" you attempt to insert into the conversation, such as sexism, classism, or capitalism, for they are distractions of denial.*

There are no exemptions. *No free passes or advanced placement. This is a required course that is either pass or fail, and the choice is up to you.*

- *If you have Black friends, colleagues, and coworkers you love, you do not get an exemption.*
- *If you are married to, dating, or have dated a Black or brown man, you are not exempt.*
- *If you have half-Black or multicultural children, there is no exemption.*
- *If you grew up in a poor, hard-working family, that does not make you exempt.*
- *If you grew up with Black people or hung out in Black neighborhoods, you are not exempt.*
- *If you have Black relatives or your best friend is Black, you do not get an exemption.*
- *If you have traveled to and/or done mission work in other countries, especially in Africa, there are no exemptions.*
- *If you live in a racially diverse neighborhood, you are not exempt.*
- *If you think you've done **enough** diversity and cultural sensitivity work, you are not exempt.*

The bottom line is that if you are White and female, there are no exemptions. Period. I think you've been ,misinformed. Somewhere along the way, you've been given the impression or taken it upon yourself to believe that any of the above scenarios make you exempt from the possibility of being racist and/or of having the entitlement of White Privilege. The truth is, if you are a White woman, you too are a White Privileged woman. As long as you live and breathe in White skin, your social and racial justice work and personal evolution will never be done. It ends only when you take your last breath. Just as my battle, my fight for equality and racial justice, never ends while in this Black skin until I take my last breath.

This will be a challenging course, no doubt. A course that will challenge you and create great stress in your life. You may reach a point where that stress becomes intolerable and triggers you to walk out, quit, give up, and never return to class. That's okay. The class will go on without you, and you'll go back to intentionally and unintentionally offending Black women you encounter. You'll go back to telling the world how feminine, sensitive, progressive, understanding, enlightening, supportive, and empowering you are to ALL women, while hurting women of color and Black women in the process. In other words, you'll go back to telling lies.

- *I will challenge your White perspective and the lens through which you view the world.*
- *I will challenge you to openly and unabashedly start talking about Whiteness and your White Identity.*
- *I will challenge your expectations of comfort and discomfort when talking about race.*
- *I will challenge you to educate yourself, and to NEVER ask women of color and Black women to educate you.*
- *I will challenge you to stop seeking White solidarity to remain in denial of your White Privilege.*
- *I will challenge you to stop claiming White Innocence; instead, I will ask you to own your privilege and use it responsibly and transformatively.*
- *I will challenge you to stop getting your cultural and racial education solely through books, movies, and the media.*
- *I will challenge you to find a group of White women who does NOT coddle you, but who instead calls you forward and stretches you.*

Lastly, I will challenge you to stand strong and not withdraw, cry, argue, defend, ignore, dismiss, attack, or retaliate in an effort to maintain your emotional balance. Your emotional equilibrium is about to be shaken, stirred, and discombobulated.

Please take your seat.

Class is now in session. Let's begin...

P.S. No, I am not angry. I am soulfully passionate about truth, freedom, healing, and justice.

P.P.S. If I were angry, I have a right to be, and you'll soon find out why.

"When you deny your White Privilege, you actively contribute to White Supremacy."

—*Catrice M. Jackson*

Chapter 1

AWAKENED TO DIFFERENCES

"We cannot change what we are not aware of, and once we are aware, we cannot help but change."

—*Sheryl Sandberg, COO of Facebook*

I sat cross-legged on the floor, my caramel-colored skin showing from the hem of my skirt to the top of my white knee-high socks, as I listened to the storyteller. Every day, we gathered in a circle on the floor, and every day, she would tell us an interesting and delightful story. I don't recall what the story was about on this particular day, but I clearly remember how story time turned into the first chapter of my personally awakened journey and life story.

It seemed like whenever it was story time, Marty would find a reason to sit next to me. I don't remember much about Marty except that he was often quite annoying, and that he served as a catalyst in my awakening simply by being his exasperating and curious self. Marty was the type of person who got on everyone's nerves; you know, the person that when you see them coming, you think, *"Oh, gosh not him again!"* Yeah. That's how Marty made just about everyone feel, including me. Not only was he annoying, but he always had something ridiculous or inappropriate to say!

Story time included an opportunity for us to ask questions.

I've always been an inquisitive person, and I loved imagining how the words of the story might come to life, like a movie in my mind. (I can see now how much of a visionary I've always been, but I didn't realize it back then.) I liked asking questions to see if the storyteller's answers would confirm or deny the vision I had created in my head. After each question was answered, the story became clearer to me, and sometimes the images I saw in my mind were totally shifted and transformed. We couldn't wait for the story to end so we could bombard the storyteller with our sometimes crazy but mostly age-appropriate questions. Today's story ended, and hands quickly went up.

Of course, Marty had a question! His hand went up over and over until he was finally called on. Every time he raised his hand, he wiggled, squirmed, and bumped into me just like an obnoxious person would. I wanted to exclaim, *"Please let him ask his question so he can stop getting on my nerves!"* Finally, his turn came. Most of us expected Marty to ask a question that had already been asked, do something to get attention, or ask a stupid question just to be annoying. That's what Marty did. That's how he behaved, always doing or saying things to get attention. But on this *never to be forgotten* day, Marty asked a deep, profound, and perplexing question that no one in the room would be able to answer, not *even* the storyteller. Marty asked a question that hurt me deep in my soul, moved me to tears, and *awakened* me in a way that I'd never experienced before.

I will never forget this moment: Marty put his stubby White hand up to his lips, spit, and then rubbed my bare leg with genuine, innocent curiosity. Before I could respond, smack the hell out of him, or push him away, he then shouted out his **life-altering question:** *"Why is Catrice so dirty?"* Everyone turned and looked at me. I looked down at my legs. The storyteller looked petrified as she sat there with her mouth hanging wide open and a beet-red face. And Marty, as serious as a heart attack, looked at the storyteller while he waited on an answer. Everyone turned to her, and I was paralyzed in place waiting on the answer too.

Time stood silently still, and it seemed like *forever* before the storyteller uttered a word. As I wiped Marty's spit off my leg and anxiously awaited her answer, I felt like I wanted to run and hide from the world. My mother was meticulous about cleanliness and quite possibly had OCD (obsessive-compulsive disorder) about being clean and making sure her kids were well put together. I always bathed, wore clean clothes, and tried to look the best I could. I didn't understand why Marty thought I was dirty. Finally, the storyteller said, *"Well Marty, Catrice is not dirty; she just has a different color of skin than you and I."* Marty looked puzzled, and I was devastated! I looked down at my legs again and realized for the first time that I was brown. **I was different.** I looked around the room to see if there was anyone who was brown like me, and it was in *that* moment I realized I was *not* like everyone else.

Marty just couldn't seem to leave it alone. He kept asking why, but the storyteller was not equipped or prepared to further answer his questions. I was six years old. It was kindergarten story time. **I was awakened.** The storyteller was our teacher, and although she was a nice woman whom I liked very much, she did not have the answers Marty or I *needed* and *wanted*. She quickly dismissed us from the story circle and told us to go to our favorite play centers. All the other kids jumped up and ran off to the painting center, the arts and crafts center, or the house center. Most of my friends went to the house center; it was our favorite. Marty scurried off to the sandbox, and I stood in the middle of the room wondering where I fit in now. My friends called me to play with them in the house center, and as I hesitantly approached them, my teacher pulled me to the side, hugged me, and said, *"Catrice, I'm sorry that happened to you earlier. You are not dirty; you're just different. Don't feel bad about that."* I was somewhat comforted by her words but still deeply unsettled. I went over to play with my friends.

I lived about six blocks from the school. At the end of that day, I found my brother and ran home so fast I don't even remember him being with me. I couldn't wait to get home to ask my mom why I was different. I cried. I told her what happened and asked, *"Why did he say I was dirty?"* I don't remember exactly what she said at the time, but she assured me I was different only because my skin was a different color, and that I was loved and special for who I was. She went on to tell me how skin color really doesn't matter, and she encouraged me to see myself beyond the color of my skin and appreciate who I was. I felt safe. But my feelings were still hurt, and I was sad. The rest is pretty much a blur. I remember going to school the next day and telling Marty to never talk to me again. He tried, but I kept telling him to leave me alone! Eventually he did. With his young, naive, and obnoxious nature, Marty served as a powerful catalyst for one of the most **painful yet purposeful** awakenings in my life.

As the school year went on, Marty quickly disappeared from my consciousness. In fact, I don't know what happened to Marty; I don't remember him being around after kindergarten. Maybe I put him so far out of my memory that he became invisible to me, or maybe he went to a different school. **But I will never ever forget this awakening.** I continued into the first and second grades without Marty in my life, and I don't recall any other skin-color-related moments that occurred while I attended Irving Elementary School. I was an outgoing, likable girl who didn't have any problems making and keeping friends. My memories after this particular awakening were mostly joyful and worth remembering for the next couple of years. Yet one thing was *forever* different: *I was different.* **My skin was brown, and to the world, I was a Black girl.** But I still felt like me on the inside, and for the most part, I felt indifferent about being different.

The summer before I entered the third grade, we moved from the North side to the West side of town. This meant I had to transfer to a new school. Back in the early 1970s, the North side was considered the "White" part of town, and the West side where I moved to was considered the "Black" side of town. I didn't understand at the time what that really meant, but there was an obvious difference. There were clearly more brown people on the West side of town, and I wasn't so different after all. Sure, there were plenty of White people in my neighborhood and many who lived on the West side of town, but for the first time, I was seeing and engaging with many different shades of brown. There were Black people, Native Americans, Hispanic people, and "light-skinned" Black people, whom I now know were biracial people. The West side felt like home. I fit in there. Many of my neighborhood friends were Native American or Black. I had a few White friends that I hung out with too. I saw the color of their skin, but at the time I didn't really "see" the color of their skin. I was still young and naive about the whole race issue, but subconsciously and consciously, I saw and embraced our differences. It really didn't matter to me what color my friends were. I would soon learn how important it is to truly SEE people.

Then it was time to go to school again, and I found out I would have to take a bus. This didn't come as a shock to me because my mother didn't really drive. Truthfully, I don't have too many memories of her driving us around. I was excited to start a new school and to ride the bus, but that changed when I realized just how far away my school was and how long the bus ride would be.

Along with a lot of other kids of color, I was bussed into yet another predominantly White school in the Crescent Park area (Crescent Park was the name of the school too). Back in the 1970s, bussing kids was the norm; it was the city's attempt to balance out the racial and ethnic segregation. I soon realized my school life would be much different than my neighborhood and home life. There were kids from various ethnic backgrounds who attended Crescent Park Elementary School, but most were Black or White.

I attended Crescent Park from third to six grades, and overall, I actually enjoyed my time there. I met some of the best people, and I am still friends with many of them. We had a Black principal, which was not heard of too often in my town, and I'll never forget him. He was a no-nonsense, hard-core disciplinarian who often showed up like a prison guard patrolling the hallways and keeping kids in check. He wasn't friendly at all, and most of the students did not like him. He prided himself on being strict and orderly. But there was something else indescribable about him. He just *seemed* to not like people in general, and my young-but-brilliant mind thought that maybe he didn't like Black people either. I clearly remember him picking on the brown and Black kids and giving us a hard time. I don't know if he *really* didn't like Black kids, or if he was trying to hold us to a higher standard. Whatever it was, it was obvious.

Over Christmas break of my fifth-grade year, when I was eleven years old, I experienced another life-altering awakening. My aunt, my mom's only sister, and my *only* aunt passed away on Christmas Eve. I remember lying in the top bunk of the bunk bed at my grandmother's house, eagerly awaiting my aunt's arrival. It was getting late, and we were all waiting for her to show up so we could get Christmas Eve started. I got my one-year-old cousin Corey (my aunt's only son), put him in the bed with me, and we took a nap.

He was sleepy, and I was already a Nanny, a natural caregiver, at such a young age. I loved babies and took every chance I could get to play with them.

I was awakened by deep painful moans and heart-wrenching cries. I could hear the grownups talking, crying, and shouting in the other room. I picked Corey up, went into the living room, and sure enough, it was true: my favorite and only Aunt Bobbie was dead. She had been found dead outside of her home. She wasn't ever going to be with us on Christmas again. I cried. I hugged Corey tight, and I told him it was going to be okay. He had no idea what was happening.

I was devastated. I felt confused and lost. I didn't know how to express my pain. I was too young to really understand death, but now I knew profoundly what losing someone to death felt like. I became bitter and angry. I had been a well-behaved child (other than being quite vocal and sassy at times), but I soon became defiant and disobedient. I didn't know what else to do. I began acting out in school, and it didn't help that my fifth-grade teacher was Mrs. Green, one of the meanest teachers in the school. *I'll never forget her, either.* She was dry, uninspiring, rigid, smart-mouthed, and strict, and I always had the feeling she didn't like teaching. She quite possibly didn't like Black kids. One day, after holding in all my sadness and frustration, and after her harassing me about what seemed to be nothing, I called her a bitch! I was quickly escorted to the principal's office. He called my mom and told her what had happened. I didn't get a chance to tell my side of the story or share why I was acting out. Back then, kids were to be seen and not heard, period!

Apparently, my behavior warranted corporal punishment. You know, when the principal has the right to spank or paddle you with a parent's permission. My mom did not play around when it came to misbehaving in school. She gave him permission to paddle me. When I think about it today, I think he enjoyed it, and even more so when he got the opportunity to paddle a *brown* kid. As I said, maybe he was trying to hold us to a higher standard, or maybe when brown kids acted out he felt like it was a bad reflection on him. Regardless, I remember him escorting me down to the lower level of the school, into the industrial broom closet. He asked me if I knew what I was getting paddled for, and although I said yes, I really didn't know why *this* form of punishment was necessary. I felt like he enjoyed swatting me three times on the butt with a paddle, which I remember being at least an inch thick with three holes in it. **Swat! Swat! Swat!** Of course I cried because it hurt, but *I also cried from the inside out because no one understood my pain.* When I got home from school, I got lectured and grounded. Needless to say, I never called a teacher a bitch again, and I struggled through fifth grade.

Third, fourth, and fifth grades at Crescent Park went by fast, and outside of a few fond and profound memories, those years seem to be a blur too. Other than my episode with Mrs. Green and the principal, I didn't have any major racial identity awakenings, problems, or monumental moments, just grade school as normal. One thing was certain: it was easy for me to make friends, and I often had a lot of them at school and in my neighborhood. I realized I had a lot of "boy" friends, and I enjoyed that.

Sixth grade is when my school-day memories become clearer. Meaningful and memorable moments were crystallized, and I soon discovered a new *difference* that took being *different* to a whole new level. I was welcomed into the sixth grade by the girls who are now known as the "mean girls." What the heck happens in the DNA of girls when they hit the sixth grade? It seems like there's a switch that turns on, and the mean girl is unconsciously activated and on full blast!

Suddenly, female friendships took on a whole new meaning and direction. I wasn't a *natural* mean girl. Sure, I had some mean-girl tendencies, but I got along with just about everyone and had no real interest in ostracizing other girls for the hell of it! When it came to making friends, race didn't usually play a factor in how my friends and I chose each other. Thanks to Marty, my eyes were forever open to the fact that my friends and classmates had different skin colors, but that really never determined the onset or quality of my friendships. What was obvious, however, although often covert, was that my friends' parents sometimes had a *problem* with me being Black. That's a whole other story in and of itself. Still, more often than not, race seemed to be toward the bottom of the qualification list. Instead, socioeconomic status reared its ugly and vivid head and never seemed to go away, starting in the sixth grade and continuing all the way through high school.

It became extremely important for girls to have the best of the best, from the type of pencils and erasers they had, to the shoes on their feet, and everything in between. It was at *this* moment I discovered the difference between "name brand" and "generic." We were poor financially. My mom had been disabled and not able to work ever since I was three or four years old. We lived on public assistance, disability, welfare, WIC, and food stamps, and my mom utilized every government program available at the time. She had to; she was a disabled single parent who did the best she could with what she had. We grew up on government commodities and Goodfellows Christmas baskets, and we didn't realize there was any other way to live. We certainly were not poor in love or spirit! My mom was a creative and resourceful genius! She knew how to care for us by doing what she called *"Stealing from Peter to pay Paul"* and *"Rubbing two nickels together to create a dollar."* I realize those are skills and gifts she's passed on to me.

My mother was artistic and had a knack for drawing, sewing, crafts, fashion, and interior design. Our homes (we moved often) were well-kept, clean, organized, and what she called "spotless." They were always nicely decorated, warm, and inviting. I always had my own room and wasn't denied any of the girly things I wanted. I dressed well, and I went to school in the best of what I had. I never really paid much attention to my clothes, hair, or shoes until I turned twelve or so, when they were brought to my attention by girls at school. I guess I've always had that *"Don't mess with me vibe,"* because it wasn't often that other girls said anything openly about how I looked or dressed. Yet I could sense they were checking me out from head to toe and analyzing my physical appearance. I was not necessarily fat, but I certainly was "bigger" than most of my friends. I have fond memories of shopping with my mom at the Goodwill and didn't realize it was a second-hand store until I got opportunities to shop at Sears, J.C. Penney, and Woolworth's. Then I clearly knew the *difference*. I had become awakened to the notion of the "haves and have nots." I definitely fit into the have nots when it came to fashion. But fashion icon or not, I was one of the "cool" girls.

It is ridiculous reflecting back on it today, but kids weren't considered "in" or "cool" if they didn't have a Hello Kitty lunch box, Strawberry Shortcake office supplies, Nike shoes, and Jordache or Sasson jeans! I know you remember those name brands if you are at all close to my age. The cool kids also wore Puma shoes, Izod polo shirts, and Levi's jeans in the sixth grade, and I rarely had those "names" in my closet. Every week, one of my girlfriends would bring some new name-brand item to school to show off, which resulted in almost every other girl running out to the store that day or shortly thereafter to buy it, too, so they could be part of the *in crowd*. I was no different. I tried to get what the other girls had when it came to school supplies, but getting name-brand clothing was a challenge due to our limited household income. I had my fair share of name-brand items over the course of sixth grade, yet deep down inside, I never really became a name-brand fanatic, and in fact, the lack thereof inspired me to create my own style. My mom was a seamstress, and she made me clothing items that were stylish and one-of-a-kind. Nevertheless, it was clear to me that money, material things, where you lived, and what your parents did for a living were top of mind for twelve- and thirteen-year-old girls.

This new sixth grade *unleashing* of the mean girl movement was pretty evident outside of the classroom too. Tetherball was the recess activity of choice back in the day. When that recess bell rang, we dashed to the tetherball square, because that's what all the *cool girls* did at recess. I was good at the game, and often won. There was little competition in that arena for me, and it didn't matter who I played against—I didn't care if my opponent was male, female, Black, White, rich, or poor. I came to win and found great pleasure in winning. Beyond the tetherball square, there were *cliques* and groups of girls creating exclusive *girl clubs*, if you will. Recess activities soon shifted from play and exercise to groups of girls getting together to gossip about and exclude other girls.

These poisonous cliques soon dominated our whole sixth grade experience. Some girls were so desperate to set themselves apart that they brought their own lunch to school in cute little sacks. **Of course they couldn't just put their damn lunch in a regular brown paper bag.** If you really wanted to be cool, you'd better bring your lunch in a cute bag and dare not eat the *poor people's free school lunch*. I occasionally brought a sack lunch to school, but let's keep it real: I liked to eat, the school lunch was pretty good, and my mom didn't have extra money for special lunch items. I must admit, there were times when I was ashamed of my bright blue, green, or yellow FREE lunch card that had to get punched by the lunch lady before I got my meal. You see, there were those who brought fancy lunch items to school in a sack lunch, those who paid fifty cents for a lunch, and then those of us who had the *dreaded FREE lunch ticket*. All these considerations were important, and something as simple as what you ate and how much it cost mattered to girls. **Boys could care less!**

Sleepovers... who didn't love spending the night at your friends' houses in grade school? I sure did and stayed over as much as my mom would let me. This is where the parents with race issues come back into play. My friends' parents loved me! I was welcome to stay at their houses whenever I wanted, and they treated me very well each time. Yet when it came time for my North side (often White) friends to come to the West side to spend the night at my house, it rarely happened. But *my girls from the block* were able to stay at my house, and I at theirs, any time we chose. It was clear that my White friends' parents **did not** want their children staying at my house, on the West side of town. Mind you, the West side of town was not a crime-ridden, drug-infested, or scary place to live. It just happened to have more Black and brown residents than any other part of town. Sure, there were sketchy neighborhoods, but we never lived in any of them. Soon our popularity was measured by whose house we stayed at and what we did while we were there. I was lucky! I was invited to the cool kids' parties and sleepovers, and I was able to hang out with my neighborhood girls too. **I lived in two different worlds and had the best of both of them.**

There was one small group of girls whose club I was never fully allowed in to. These were the White daughters of doctors, dentists, and other prestigious community positions. I remember one girl in particular; everyone wanted to be friends with her. She was the daughter of a dentist and definitely carried herself like a rich kid. She was cool with me at school and was in my sixth-grade class, but outside of the classroom she was clearly not interested in creating a stronger relationship. If you got invited to her house and her parties you knew you had made it into the *elite clique*. I was one who didn't get *the* invitation. Part of me secretly wanted to be invited, and the other part of me didn't care.

Bragging about how much money parents made, bringing your own cute sack lunch, sporting the latest styles, flashing name-brand symbols on this and that, left and right, and judging others based on what part of town they lived in became the *sixth-grade way of life* for many girls. This soon led to ridiculing others because of the kind of car their parents drove; whether they were fat or skinny, cute or ugly; or whether they were popular or unpopular with the boys. The mean girl movement was in full force, and I knew this sixth-grade moment was just the tip of the *infamous popularity contest iceberg*.

I must admit that I was both victim and perpetrator in some of the schoolgirl games. I hurt other girls for no reason, and I was hurt by them for the same stupid reasons. I'm sure this ridiculous and painful behavior is part of the nature of the preteen beast and that it is still occurring in schools and playgrounds all over the world. It's even worse today with the access to social media and cyberbullying. These painful moments certainly shape who we become as women, especially if a girl has low self-esteem to begin with. There was one part of this mean girl movement that I **refused** to take part in. As we prepared to transition into what was then called junior high school, it became popular to be a girl who *made out and put out* with boys. That's where I drew the line! **There was no way in hell I was going to give up my virginity or let a boy fondle me just to be cool and be a member of the**

cool kids' club. It wasn't happening, no way, no how, period! I had absolutely no interest in sex, and quite frankly, I was afraid of it. Many of my friends in the sixth grade had already been to *third* and *fourth base* with boys. Instead of seeing them as cool, I saw them as disgusting, and truth be told, the boys did too—after they got what they wanted.

Wow! Look at all this psychological drama occurring even before we women officially become teenagers. **It's sad, it's reality, and it happens every day.** The gossiping, judging, hating, ridiculing, excluding, and ostracizing that happens in the sixth grade and continues into high school still runs rampant today, and the *pitiful truth* is, **it's happening among grown-ass women on the playground called "the women's empowerment arena,"** smack dab in the middle of the *so-called* **feminist movement.** That's right, many women are behaving just like they did in the sixth grade, and the only differences between then and now are the *types* of games being played.

Are you a perpetrator, victim, bystander, or a combination of all three? Are you playing sixth-grade schoolgirl games in a full-grown woman's body? Are you deciding whether to play with another female based on whether or not she has Hello Kitty folders? Are you consciously or unconsciously leading an exclusive movement, or are you a ring leader in the mean girl's movement? Does the way a woman dresses, speaks, looks, or who she hangs out with determine whether she is qualified or disqualified to play on *your* playground? Do you actively engage in *Cliques, Catfights,* and *Colorblindness* as a grown woman? Are you like the parents of my childhood friends, saying you **don't see color**, class, race, or ethnicity, but you *really* do—and you deny or minimize them? **Do you have conscious and/or unconscious "race issues" that harm women of color and Black women?** If you are brutally honest with yourself, the answer to at least one of these questions will be yes!

We've come a long way, but there is so much more progress to be made in the women's empowerment movement. The greatest change and transformation in this arena will begin with you. Because the way I see it—based on my vantage point and my life experiences—you are an *Antagonist, Advocate,* or *Ally* for other women. You may play a bit of each role, but one is your predominant role, and it's time for you to discover which one you are and be the change you talk about. At a peace conference in 2009, the Dalai Lama said, *"The world will be saved by the Western woman."* I wholeheartedly agree with what the Dalai Lama said, and I will add to his sentiment: "Women *won't save the world* until they heal themselves and stop excluding and hurting other women."

I'm different. You're different. So what! Let's shine the light on those differences, respect them, honor them, embrace them, and celebrate them. We've got more important things to address and accomplish than to be worrying about Hello Kitty and Strawberry Shortcake. **It's time to walk the damn talk and truly BE the change we talk about and so desperately need.** The world is waiting on us to heal ourselves and then to save it. Let the **Awakened Conscious Shift begin!**

WAKE-UP CALL QUESTIONS

Are you using your White Privilege to help or harm women of color and Black women?

_____

_____

_____

_____

What schoolgirl games are you still playing?

_____

_____

_____

_____

What "type" of women are you excluding, and why?

_____

_____

_____

_____

_____

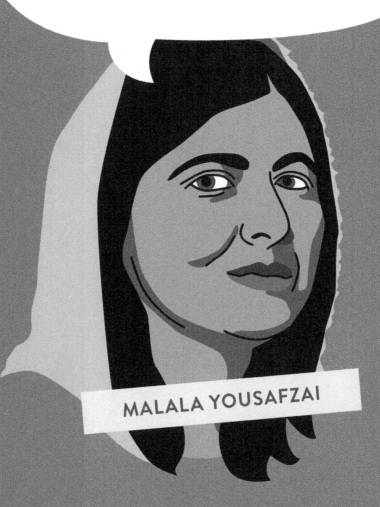

Chapter 2

THE MYSTERIOUS WESTERN WOMAN

"There will never be a new world order until women are a part of it."

—Alice Paul

So, what did the Dalai Lama really mean when he said, *"The world will be saved by the Western woman"*? Who are the Western women, and how will they save the world? I actually took the time to Google "Who are Western women" and made some surprising discoveries. According to Urban Dictionary, *"A western woman is a woman who is difficult and stressful. She also hates how Asian women are often happy being subservient to men."* Whoa! I certainly wasn't expecting that. Urban Dictionary went on to share some of the top words associated with Western women, including "bitch," "feminism," "modern woman," "receptacle," and "White woman." I knew there had to be a better definition, so I kept looking. I found an interesting post on Yahoo Answers; according to them, Western women are women who:

- *Live in Western countries (or who live in North America, Australia, or Europe)*
- *Are not Muslim*
- *Have total freedom of speech and freedom of expression*

Of course, there were comments and answers that bashed the Western woman by identifying her as "man-hating," "privileged," "egotistical," and other negative characteristics.

I had never researched Western women before, and I was amazed by everything I was finding. Still, I knew there had to be more, so I Googled "What did the Dalai Lama mean by the Western woman will save the world." Several blog sites came up, and I read several of them, but I still couldn't find a definitive definition of who Western women are. Many of the blog posts suggested that the Western woman is the *divine feminine*, the empowered woman, and/or women who have access to power, education, money, and influence, but no real definition was forthcoming. I remained puzzled and perplexed, so I decided to post this question on my personal Facebook page: *"WHO are Western women? The Dalai Lama said the world will be saved by the Western woman? Who is she? Who are they?"* Slowly the comments started coming in. Here's a compilation of the answers I received:

- *We are the Western women because we live in the Western hemisphere.*
- *I think the Dalai Lama is referring to women like us in Western countries who have the freedom to be big in the world and take action.*
- *It's women with compassion along with freedom in the West, versus women in other countries who have no voice or rights.*
- *The Western women are strong women who make their own way in the world, women who choose to believe in their strength and vision, women like Gloria Steinem, Oprah Winfrey, and Hillary Clinton.*

- *The Western women are women who step out of patriarchy and step into the true role of early healers who are deeply connected with the rhythms and cycles of Mother Earth.*
- *The Western woman is from an industrialized country, and she can do things for herself and collaborate with others. She is a visionary woman who has choices and freedom, and who uses her power to empower others.*

Their definitions and comments made sense to me on a cognitive level. However, my intuition was telling me that *something, someone* was missing. Truthfully, I'd felt like there was something missing ever since I first heard the Dalai Lama's legendary statement in 2011.

Ironically, a short time after hearing the Dalai Lama's statement being used as a "call" for women around the world to step into their *feminine power* by many in the women's empowerment arena, I was referred by a past colleague to be considered for a collaborative book project. After a few email exchanges, I was invited to participate, and I received the contributor guidelines for the project. A very nice woman named Caroline sent me the following description of what the book was about and what was required from each contributor:

> *"The idea with this book is to celebrate women, feminine values, and the female spirit. Examples of feminine characteristics include cooperation/collaboration, nurturing/motherhood, receptivity, compassion, and intuition (and others). Through your personal experiences, we will engage these questions: What makes women valuable and an essential part of humanity? What is our impact? How do women and feminine values help the world?"*

I was quite excited about being part of this project, and felt I had a valuable contribution to make regarding the importance of women collaborating with one another. I reviewed the information, submitted my chapter idea, and was selected to be one of the coauthors for *Women Will Save the World*. Giddy with excitement, I said yes to sharing my truth in two thousand words or less.

Before I agreed to participate in this project, I inquired about the other women who were involved in it. I wanted to know who I was collaborating with; I wanted to know if we had similar business values, especially from a branding point of view. It turned out that although I was familiar with a few of the women through social media, I personally knew only two of them. Still, I agreed to participate and began working on my chapter. After a few weeks, I submitted the final version of my chapter, titled "Collaborating to Create Change the Feminine Way."

Here's what I wrote:

It wasn't until my late thirties that I discovered the concept of the feminine and stopped thinking, feeling, and showing up in the world in masculine ways. You see, for most of my life, I thought being feminine meant being soft, weak, docile, dependent, and submissive. I had no idea that true femininity held a power and a strength all its own.

As a child, the absence of positive male role models in my life convinced me I had no time to be soft. Like my mother, grandmother, and aunts, I had to be strong and take care of myself. Not yet understanding true feminine strength, I thought this meant I had to be tough and go it alone. In short, I thought I had to act like a man.

As a result, I consciously chose to be independent and take charge of my life. While I physically looked feminine and took great interest in looking my best, I didn't feel feminine on the inside. Before I knew it, I had morphed into a tough, outspoken female who didn't take any crap from anyone! At the time, I was proud of who I was becoming because I thought I was standing in my power. I didn't recognize then how much I had to learn about what that meant.

Alienated from my own feminine nature, I became alienated from other females as well. During my junior high and high school years, I watched other girls as they used their outward appearance to seek, attract, and get boys, as they developed cliques and groups that ostracized others, and as they gossiped about and backstabbed each other. Competition seemed to be the name of the game, and I didn't want to participate in it. I didn't fully understand what was happening among us as girls then, but I knew—at a soul level—that it didn't feel right for me.

Though I wasn't overly competitive, I didn't understand the meaning of feminine collaboration. I didn't feel like I had anything in common with other girls. I had drawn the conclusion that girls (women) were catty, messy, and hateful. In fact, I intentionally kept my circle of female friends small and enjoyed hanging out with male friends more often.

But something felt wrong. Somewhere deep inside of me I longed for deeper, soulful connections with women. I realize now that as teenage girls we all were either clueless about the power of being in our feminine or were driven by the power of being masculine. I realize we had no idea the pain, drama, and confusion we were creating in the lives of each other and of ourselves.

At 32 years old, I moved to a new city and started a women's support group out of my home. Though I was a mental health counselor, I had avoided emotional connection with women for most of my life. Opening my home and my heart to these women felt like a big risk for me, but I was convinced I had something to teach them.

To my surprise, I became the student! I learned they were no different than me. I saw them in me and me in them. As I looked into their souls, I saw my own soul with new, loving eyes.

These women, whom I had imagined would gain so much from me, ended up teaching me how to share without shame and to be vulnerable enough to speak the truth even if I was afraid. Most importantly, they taught me that when women unite and create a sacred community of support, we can heal ourselves, our families, and the world, one woman at a time. Something within my soul was awakened. From somewhere deep inside, I heard a small voice softly say, "Welcome home, again."

It wasn't the first time I had heard that voice—the voice of my soul reminding me I am a daughter of the feminine. I had heard it before, but it had been a long time since I had experienced the feeling. Suddenly, it felt good to remember the truth.

Later, in 1996, I had the opportunity to work as an AmeriCorps volunteer at a local domestic violence and sexual assault shelter. For three years, I advocated for, educated, counseled, and supported women survivors of abuse. Within months of taking the position, my soul was inspired and awakened to the movement of women's empowerment; it was something I had never experienced before. I loved every minute of my work, and I immediately knew it was what I was created to do on a soul level: to liberate, inspire, and empower the lives of women.

Unfortunately, although the job felt heaven-sent, the environment often reminded me of my teenage years. Though I worked with some amazing and passionate women who deeply cared about transforming the lives of women, ironically the *environment was filled with competition, ego, and selfishness. We could not get ourselves out of the way to soulfully create the change we so desired to create. It was confusing—but I hoped there was a better way. On some unexplainable level deep within, I knew that, with simple faith, a power greater than us could facilitate the change we desired.*

Sometime after, I began work at yet another women's empowerment program. For two years, I worked for a national women's program in my local community. Again, I loved it. Again, I heard my inner voice tell me I was home. Still, though I thoroughly enjoyed the work, the competitive and sometimes destructive actions of the other women—who were supposed to be working together for the greater good—was too much for me.

In early December 2007, my soul's calling finally hit me—like a ton of bricks! During a routine doctor's visit, I discovered my hemoglobin count was 5.5, with the normal range for women being 12-16. My vital organs were not getting enough oxygen, and I was, in the words of my doctor, "walking dead."

My soul battled between the words of my late grandmother, who had taught me it was a sin to take body parts from another human being, and my spirit, which knew I had a purpose to fulfill and a destiny to live. I experienced what I call a Soul Eruption, a deep and profound moment when you know for sure who you are and why you are here.

Afraid, I prayed and chose to take the blood, vowing to God that I would live and fully carry out His calling for my life. I made a soul commitment to live the rest of my life pioneering a global movement that would liberate, inspire, and empower women.

I left the hospital on a Friday, contemplated my life all day Saturday, and on Sunday sat down and wrote a resignation letter that would be the beginning of my life's work as it is today. On

Monday, I submitted the letter with no fear or regret. In fact, it was one of the most soul-liberating experiences of my life. I left the organization to pursue my soul dream of becoming an entrepreneur, who speaks and coaches to inspire women on my own terms.

I knew then that all of my life lessons and experiences with women—good, bad, and indifferent—happened for a reason. They were preparation for my plan and purpose to teach and inspire women to come together without shame or fear, to create a soul community where women could embrace their feminine selves to connect and collaborate, to heal the lives of women around the world. I didn't know exactly how or when this would occur, but I trusted in the why and used what God gave me to lead women into their feminine greatness.

It has been five years since then. Five years in which I have been seeking to deeply understand and embrace the beauty of the feminine. I've come to know that it is our most powerful space to be in as women. We were created to love, nurture, create, commune, co-create, and collaborate within communities to care for, inspire, and heal humanity. While we must seek harmony among our feminine and masculine energies, when we live from, operate within, and engage with others from our feminine source, we are being all that we were created to be.

Competition amongst women takes us out of the natural flow of life. When we compete with one another, there is strife, struggle, and resistance; we are driven by our egos to conquer instead of connecting and collaborating. There are times when we must be driven, focused, strong, and in charge, but not to the extent that we hurt others and lack compassion for the human spirit.

Universally, there is no reason to compete. You are enough, I am enough, and there is enough for all of us. Once I soulfully digested this truth, I gracefully could stand in the power of my feminine and honor the feminine within other women. Amazing things happen when we do this.

My life's journey has taught me the significant difference between being a woman and living in the feminine. In my opinion, living as a woman is a physical manifestation; living from our feminine is a soul experience anchored in who we innately are. Living in the feminine and collaborating from this space allows us to care for ourselves, care for others, and impact the world with the collective power of connectedness and compassion. Choosing feminine collaboration in our lives, work, and mission decreases competition, lessens the struggle, and affords us more ease and grace. As we travel our journey, I share with you a perspective to consider as you consciously embrace your feminine self:

When a woman steps into her feminine, she realizes that her soul is the most beautiful part of who she is. When a woman deeply discovers her feminine, she honors the essence of who she is from the inside out. When a woman embraces her feminine, she soulfully knows she is embracing the feminine souls of women around the world. When a woman owns her feminine, she embodies her innate ability to care for, love, and nurture all who enter her space, especially herself. When a woman honors her feminine, she is not afraid to be comforting, compassionate, sensual, and soft for fear of being seen as weak. When a woman engages in her feminine, she honors the feminine in other women and creates communities where the feminine is celebrated and not tolerated. When a woman leads from her feminine, she blazes the trail of her destiny by shining the light of her soul, thus creating a path for other women to follow.

We are the pulse of the world, and when we live from our feminine, we pulsate powerful vibrations that echo beyond what we can imagine. The feminine spirit of collaboration is at the core of who we are; to engage in contrast weakens our collective vibration. When we come together as women with the pure intention to collaborate, to create greater good, we not only heal and empower ourselves, we enhance and transform the human experience.

I hope you choose to let go of insecurity, shame, fear, and judgment. I hope you choose to see and honor the feminine in other women. I hope you choose to go forth knowing with every cell of your body that you are enough, she is enough, we are enough, just the way we are. I challenge you to trust in your value and your gifts with full confidence and to know that there is no competition because there is enough for all of us.

—Catrice M. Jackson, "Collaborating to Create Change the Feminine Way," from Women Will Save the World, Caroline A. Shearer

I was extremely pleased with my message and believed it would enlighten, inspire, and empower a lot of women. Finally, the day came when I received my copy of the book in the mail. **I was beyond thrilled to have participated in a project with a message I believe in, that *women* WILL save the world.**

The time came for us to promote the book and share it with the world. For the first time, I was actually able to connect a bit deeper with the other contributors and put faces with names. After rushing to the newly designed website for the book, I saw a beautiful page dedicated to the book's contributors. I first scrolled down to see my own picture and bio. Come on, you know you would have done the same! There I was. What a meaningful moment of joy I experienced. I went back up to the top and began reading the biographies of my fellow contributors. They all appeared to be amazing, heart-centered, and extraordinary women. I felt proud to be among such brilliance. And then, my joy began to be replaced with disappointment. *Something, someone* was missing from that fabulous web page.

I knew *exactly* what was missing. **The same thing I have always felt was missing.** I read each bio intentionally. I looked at each woman's photo deeply. I scrolled up. I scrolled down, and then back up to the top again, searching for—well, truthfully, I was searching for more women who looked like me. More women who looked different from the majority of the women I saw on the website. At first glance, all the contributors except for me and one other woman *appeared* to be White. Being White certainly did not discredit the women from sharing valuable information, nor did it discount their compassion for the world. **But I wondered, why weren't the voices and messages of a diverse group of women selected for a book like this?** I don't really know the race or ethnicity of the other women, but I was sure of one thing, all but one didn't look like me. They didn't look African, Indian, Native American, Asian, or even another shade of brown.

So, back to my search for the answer to *"Who are the Western women?"* When I had posted my question on Facebook, I had received only fifteen or so comments, and all but one of the comments were made by White women. I found this interesting as well. My personal friend list on Facebook is pretty diverse, and I often get more comments from my African American friends, but not on this particular post. And I'm intrigued how Caroline (the woman who led the *Women Will Save the World* book project) determined who she would select for her book project. It seems as though she reached out to women she knew personally and also asked them for referrals. I never asked her what her process was.

The end result is what matters. At first glance, the contributors she chose for her book project mostly looked like her: White women. I'm not even sure if *she* is aware of this obvious observation.

Not too long after the release of Caroline's book, *Women Will Save the World,* another book was released with a similar title: *Wonder Women: How Western Women Will Save the World.* This book was written by Jessica Eaves Mathews and Phil Dyer, and it eventually became a number one Amazon bestseller. Although I haven't read the book, I am sure it contains valuable information as well.

There is a reason I never read the book nor had any interest in doing so. The book's cover features a White-appearing woman who is pulling open her suit jacket in Clark Kent fashion to reveal the book's title. You know how Clark Kent transformed into Superman by pulling open his shirt? Yes, that's what the woman on the cover is doing . Now you may be wondering why this image caused me to have no interest in the book. And you may even believe that my choice sounds like the *"Don't judge a book by its cover"* cliché. You would be correct. **Let's just keep it real.** We all judge books and people by their covers, and if you say you don't, you are lying to yourself. **It's human nature. It's instinctive. It's a gut reaction. It's the truth. It isn't fair, but it happens all the time.**

We all see *differences.* Glaring differences or subtle differences, it doesn't matter—we can't help but see and feel them. There's nothing wrong with seeing differences. **Wrong happens when we begin to treat people differently because of their differences.** The observation in and of itself is basic human nature. I'll be talking more about differences throughout this book.

So back to this particular book cover. Again, the title is *Wonder Women: How Western Women Will Save the World.* The main image on the cover is a woman who appears to be White and who is wearing a suit. The cover didn't speak to me for those simple reasons: I'm not a White woman, and I'm not a woman in corporate America who wears a suit. I struggled with whether this particular book was written with *me* in mind and/or whether it would speak to my Intersectionality. That's a topic I'll be talking about in Chapter Six, but essentially, I wondered if the book would address issues and challenges of *race and gender*. I am both of those: I am Black, I am a woman. I am a Black woman. Every day I live and breathe in a feminine, female Black body. I cannot escape either one, nor do I choose to. Oh! You didn't realize that I AM a Black woman? How did you not see that obvious difference?

I decided to check out the book's description and reviews on the authors' website. You can certainly go check out the book for yourself and maybe you'll be intrigued enough to read it, but just in case, this is part of its description:

> "Providing a blunt diagnosis for the cause of the extensive problems in our economy (fueled by the testosterone-laden, traditional approach to business), the book outlines how women (and men) can stage a recovery with a focus not just on the bottom line, but on bringing humanity and empathy back to business. There is a seismic shift taking place today in the way businesses are launched, how they are run and—most importantly—in how success is measured. The traditional business model, fueled by testosterone and focused on winning at all costs, is irretrievably broken. Further, many of the devastating problems we now see in our country and the world today are a direct result of this mindset taken to the extreme. Fortunately, a movement is underway... *a movement toward a better way of life and a better career. One based in a better*

wayofdoingbusiness—onebasedinthenurturing,relationship-centeredfeminineenergy. And this shift is being led by women like you. These Wonder Women are upturning societal and business norms and making the business 'streets' safe again for all citizens, women and men alike. They are poised to step into their power and to help bring the rest of the world along with them. And not a moment too soon. Our future depends on it. As the Dalai Lama stated, *'The world will be saved by the Western Woman.'*"

Once I read the book's description and most of the reviews, I decided it was not a book I was interested in reading. I'm sure it's a good book, but it didn't pique my interest. What I did find interesting in the description were the last several sentences: "They are poised to step into their power and to help bring the rest of the world along with them. And not a moment too soon. Our future depends on it. As the Dalai Lama stated, *'The world will be saved by the Western Woman.'*" And that caused me once again to wonder, who is this Western woman people keep referring to? Is the Western woman the woman on this book cover? Is she the women shown on the *Women Will Save the World* book's website? **Who is she?**

Let's cut to the chase. We don't know who the Dalai Lama was referring to in his landmark, inspiring, partially true, blanket statement. Has anyone ever asked him? Has he given a definitive answer? If he has, I missed it. In the meantime, women and men have begun to formulate their own definitions, and **I don't believe those definitions really include women of color and Black women.** In fact, I don't believe a woman of color has written a book claiming she is included in the Dalai Lama's proclamation. I'm still searching for such a book because I would love to hear other perspectives. If you are a woman of color, do you feel included? If you are a White woman, do visions of strong, powerful, change-generating women of color come to mind when you hear the words "Western women"? When you reflect on the Dalai Lama's statement, do iconic women like Oprah Winfrey, Angela Davis, Michelle Obama, or Iyanla Vanzant come to mind? Do you see Asian, Muslim, Indian, and Latina women? Do you think your neighbors or colleagues of color are included in this definition? **Who *is* this mysterious Western woman?** Are you one? Am I one? The Dalai Lama made this bold statement at the Vancouver Peace Summit 2009. Much of the world respects his wisdom, and so I think it's essential that women KNOW who he was talking about, that we know who the Western woman is. Aren't you just a *little* curious about who he is referring to? I definitely am. We need to figure out who she is so she can save the world!

WAKE-UP CALL QUESTIONS

Be honest. What kind of women did NOT come to mind when you heard the Dalai Lama's proclamation? Why? What is that all about?

_____

_____

_____

_____

_____

In what ways, directly and indirectly, are you excluding, failing to invite, or bypassing women of color and Black women?

_____

_____

_____

_____

_____

_____

_____

When you say you empower ALL women, do you really? What's your plan to become intentionally inclusive of women of color and Black women?

_____

_____

_____

_____

_____

_____

_____

Chapter 3

THE ANTAGONIST

"You can do one of two things; just shut up, which is something I don't find easy, or learn an awful lot very fast, which is what I tried to do."

—*Jane Fonda*

I can tell you for sure who is NOT the Western woman, and yes, I will boldly call her out: **The Antagonist**. You might be an Antagonist. You might have experienced the attitude and wrath of the Antagonist. Truthfully, at some point we've all been the Antagonist. The question is, will you continue to be an Antagonist? And another is, will you unleash the courage to confront her when she shows up in your life, whether that means confronting yourself or someone else who is antagonizing other women? So, while we're still cultivating a definitive definition of the Western woman, the definition of the antagonistic woman is undeniable: she is a woman who "actively opposes or is hostile to someone or something" (*Oxford English Dictionary*); she makes everything difficult and challenging; she is defensive, argumentative, and aggressive; she seems to enjoy inserting drama into every situation; and she blames and/or excludes others. Do you know someone like that? She would be the perfect poster child for the *mean girl* campaign!

Whose face comes to mind when you hear that description? I'm sure at least one does, but have you considered it might be you? It may be time to take a closer look in the mirror. In the women's empowerment arena, the Antagonist shows up a bit differently. If you're not careful, you might mistake her for a conscious champion for women, but **do not be fooled, not everything that shines is gold.** In fact, many Antagonists perceive themselves to be highly conscious of the needs, desires, and challenges of women, until the challenges of race, ethnicity, and Intersectionality are introduced into the discussion. Ah yes, the forbidden topic of race and all the personal and social barriers and challenges that come along with it. Many women leaders are educated, well-versed, and equipped to intercede and empower other women when it comes to gender disparities, but not as many are endowed with the insight, education, compassion, and experience to intercede at the crossroads between gender and race.

Truthfully, many of these same leaders are unaware that they are ill-prepared for *"race talks,"* and many dread the whole damn conversation! I have experienced this *lack of concern and preparedness* many times in my life, but let me highlight a moment that stands out among the rest. Before you conclude that this is an isolated event and/or that this experience is a figment of my imagination, consider this: *What if it IS true?* **That is one of the critical questions you must ask yourself as you read this book, because this book's message is about hearing, valuing, and honoring the truths of your fellow sisters.** If you are unwilling to ask this question, then you are not interested in—or a champion of—*true* sisterhood. And just because you can't hear, find, or understand the truth in someone else's experience STILL does not mean it's not true. So as you continue to read this book, keep asking yourself, *"What if this is true?"*

The moment I will share with you occurred with "Denise," a woman I was connected to on Facebook. Denise appeared to not only have a fairly large following of women, but was also considered a "leader" in the women's empowerment arena. Women generally seemed to adore her, and she often garnered quite a bit of conversation and engagement in her social media posts. One day in April of 2015, I noticed a post she made about the race-related riots happening in Baltimore, Maryland. As a socially conscious woman and social justice activist, these types of posts always catch my attention; however, I rarely respond to them anymore, because quite frankly, I expect White women to always respond the same way that Denise and her friends did in this example.

Her post read something like this:

"I'm appalled at what's happening in Baltimore. There are youth in school uniforms running wild, looting, stealing, and throwing bricks at police officers. The violence and their laughter is disturbing. This is not justice for Freddie Gray! These youth are not protestors. They are criminals taking advantage of the pain and loss the family of Freddie Gray is experiencing on the day they lay him to rest."

I was emotionally struck not by the post itself, but by the **choice of words she used to describe the youth** and by the fact that many women echoed her disdain. Let me be clear: I do NOT condone violence or anything that perpetuates violence. Just stick with me for a moment and you'll hear my perspective more clearly.

Who is Freddie Gray? Freddie Carlos Gray Jr. was a twenty-five-year-old African American man arrested by the Baltimore police for having an illegal switchblade in his possession. While he was being transported in a police van to the police station, he allegedly fell into a coma and was taken to the trauma center. It was later revealed that he died of spinal cord injuries that occurred during transport. Six Baltimore police were temporarily suspended with pay. They were eventually indicted for using unnecessary force while arresting him, and criminal charges were filed for murder. The medical examiner ruled Gray's death a homicide. There were eyewitnesses who reported that unnecessary force had been used; thus, the community was in an uproar about yet another death/ homicide of a Black man at the hands of police.

The city was set ablaze with protestors and yes, rioters and looters. A major protest turned violent on April 25, 2015; many were arrested and fifteen police officers were injured. On April 27, 2015, the day of Freddie's funeral, the civil unrest intensified, which eventually resulted in the governor declaring a state of emergency and calling in the National Guard.

So, back to the Facebook post fiasco! I commented on Denise's post and asked her why she couldn't understand the rioting, and all hell broke loose from there. I don't condone rioting just for the sake of rioting, and violence in any form is never good; however, I understood *why* so many people were upset, and *why* they were rioting and protesting in the streets of Baltimore. If you're familiar with this moment in Baltimore, the rioting is **not** what this situation with my Facebook "friend" was about.

Shortly after my question, the foolery floodgates swung open! One of Denise's friends, who appeared to be a White woman, said, *"The majority of violence in the United States and Canada is caused by Black men."*

I responded with, *"Where did you get that statistic?"*

She answered, *"I don't need facts; I'm entitled to my opinion."*

I agreed with her; she is entitled to her opinion. I also stated that when she is accused of being racially biased, I hope she owns that as well. I shared that as a mother of a twenty-two-year-old Black son, I was offended by her comment. She didn't care. She kept protecting her right to express her racially biased opinion.

Then another of Denise's friends, who also appeared to be White, went on and on about how she hates Al Sharpton, how much of a pot stirrer he is, and that he is a culprit in the nationwide racial and social unrest. My response to her was that Al Sharpton is a scapegoat; he is not the real problem. Then a woman with brown skin stated, *"There is a lot of racial bias in Baltimore, so let's focus on that and not on Al Sharpton."* Other White-appearing women inserted their comments, adding fuel to the fire. In the meantime, Denise was silently watching all this happen to her post. And then… she finally spoke.

Her response was amazingly typical. She said, *"You know what I love about you guys, that we can come together and talk to each other without being disrespectful, thank you so much!"* Seriously? Are you kidding me? **Did she miss all the racist verbal vomit and discriminatory dialogue that just happened?** She went on to respond to my previous comment about having a Black son and not appreciating him being stereotyped by saying, *"Catrice, I sure hate that a lot of my Black friends feel this way and want you to know that I will always do what I can to bring positive change when I can."* Denise then posted that someone had called her a racist on Twitter as a result of the same initial Facebook post. More craziness was unleashed, and she said, *"If I dare speak up as a White chick, I'm called a racist, and I won't tolerate that."*

My response to her was exactly this: *"It's not about you speaking up as a White chick. It's about allowing your 'friends' to make such statements and NOT addressing them. It sends the impression that you agree."* Shit hit the fan!

But instead of sharing all the racially charged, insensitive, immature, and unconscious comments that followed, I will condense what transpired during this Facebook conversation between my "friend" Denise and me. Denise expressed that she had had very deep talks with women regarding race issues in the past, and she did not believe that just because a person is of a certain race (White) that they are responsible for the injustices carried out by other White people. Denise felt strongly that she is NOT the White generations who came before her, and when people of color used the terminology *"her people"* (referring to White people), it offended her.

I agreed that she was not the past generations of White people, but that she **does** in fact benefit from the privileges passed down to her from those past generations. I added she cannot just ignore that truth.

She then responded to something I had said earlier in the conversation. *"Catrice, it is about me speaking up as a White woman in many cases, how can you say it is not?"* She suggested that I ask her direct questions because "inference is a dangerous thing." I answered that the whole discussion thread was full of inference; it had started with an inference and then several inferring comments came flooding in. In my opinion, Denise's initial post had reeked with inference, which is why I responded to it in the first place.

Let me remind you of Denise's post:

*"I'm appalled at what's happening in Baltimore. There are youth in school uniforms running wild, looting, stealing, and throwing bricks at police officers. The violence and their laughter is disturbing. This is not justice for Freddie Gray! These youth are not protestors. **They are criminals** taking advantage of the pain and loss the family of Freddie Gray is experiencing on the day they lay him to rest."*

I put the words *"They are criminals"* in boldface for a reason. **Any time people of color finally get sick and damn tired of the oppressive system of racism that kills them emotionally, psychologically, or literally, and begin to fight back, they are dehumanized and labeled with words like "criminal," "thug," "monsters," and so on.** When White people get tired, run wild, loot, or behave badly in public, words like "rowdy" and "spirited" are attached to their *behavior*. Pay close attention here. **The words used to describe people of color are insults and personal attacks. The words used to describe uncontrollable White people attack their behavior.** There is a distinct difference, and if you wake up and pay attention, you'll begin to see it too. From my perspective, Denise's initial post was clearly an attack on Black *people* and not on the behaviors they were demonstrating. It was an attack that I've seen countless times, and that's why I sought clarification by asking Denise why she couldn't understand the reasons for the rioting. I wasn't agreeing or disagreeing with rioting. I wanted to know if she had a deeper understanding of what was *really* happening in Baltimore. In my opinion, her initial post began with "inference" because she labeled the youth as *criminals*.

Maybe you too would label them criminals, and maybe you wouldn't. The challenge question is, if these were White people behaving badly in the street, what would you think or say? Let me give you an example of how this double standard plays out in real life and in the media. The headline reads, *"Nine dead in Texas biker brawl!"* Google this for yourself and you'll discover more. On May 17, 2015, less than thirty days after the "rioting" that took place in Baltimore, a bikers' *brawl* resulting in nine casualties and various injuries occurred in Texas. Five different gangs were involved in this incident in Waco, Texas. These White folks engaged in a real life *Wild Wild West* shootout in the middle of town over a petty argument, and then they audaciously turned their gunfire onto the police. Over and over again in the media coverage, these *murderers* were described as participating in a brawl! In several accounts, the brawl was referred to as a "gunfight." **They weren't called criminals, monsters, killers, assassins, or terrorists, yet nine people died in Waco, Texas that day.** The National Guard wasn't called in. The K-9 units weren't dispatched. The brawlers were not attacked with tear gas. Nope, none of that happened. Why? My point is this. White people set cities on fire after professional sporting events, White people get drunk and act like fools in the streets, and White people who express anger or discontent are defined as people who simply just lost control in a *brawl* or got a little too *rowdy*! Okay, so I digressed, but it was necessary to make my point. Start paying attention. You'll see it if you're open to seeing it.

After I brought up the fact that Denise's initial post started the inference, she responded with, *"Catrice, what do you think I am inferring?"* Then she said, *"Catrice, by 'inference' are you saying that you are able to infer what others are saying in their posts? And if you are, it is you that has the problem because I'm reading the posts and they seem clear to me."* She continued to shift the focus and insisted that I was the one with the "inference problem." She defended every post made by her friends regardless of whether they were racially biased, unfounded, or simply disrespectful. Denise was not able to see how her labeling the rioters as "criminals" was an inference. She continued to defend her friend who made the blanket and racially biased statement that *"most crimes in the United States are committed by Black men."* Denise did not see anything wrong with that statement, and while she agreed it might have been wrong for her friend to say, and possibly inaccurate, the statement was NOT racially biased. She then suggested that we focus on the current moment and work together to make the world a place where we all feel equal.

I responded with a question I hoped would create a breakthrough: *"What if I said that ALL White women were weak and docile?"*

Denise said, *"I would ask you where you got that information from; is this your opinion and do you believe this is true?"*

I tried to show Denise how my blanket statement about White women was similar to her friend's blanket statement about Black men creating crimes. Denise could not understand, and she finally asked, *"If my friend's statement had been backed by statistics, would it still have been considered racially biased?"* **Are you exhausted by all this yet? Is it hard to follow? Are you agreeing or disagreeing? Well hang on, I'm about to wrap this up for you.**

Just when I was about to walk away and call it quits, one of Denise's other White friends, who I'll call "Teresa," chimed in with a breath of fresh air. Teresa posted, *"What Denise's friend posted IS racist, and you are being way too nice about it, Catrice!"* **I felt like I had been drowning in the sea all by myself and someone had finally thrown me a life jacket.** Teresa gave me a much needed *break* from the same ol' fight, from the Racial Battle Fatigue, of trying to get White women to see another perspective when it comes to issues of race. Prior to Teresa showing up on the scene, every White woman involved in the discussion refused to see any other perspective and blatantly denied that any racism was taking place. Teresa showed up as an Advocate, for sure!

In the meantime, Denise returned to the conversation with some statistics and a link to an article that basically stated that what her friend posted about Black men being responsible for most crimes was incorrect. In fact, it stated that more White people commit crimes. However, she continued to state that I was the one "inferring," that I had the problem, and that people of color can be racist too. I told her she was a *privileged* White woman who would have difficulty seeing it from my perspective. I encouraged her to become educated on White Privilege and how she benefits from it, and then she might begin to see the racism in this particular discussion. She candidly told me she disagreed with me, did not appreciate my accusations or my **tone**, and finally, that she was not interested in learning from my "inferences."

Denise told me to take my offensive comments and unjust accusations to my space because they were not welcome in her space. And lastly, she informed me that I was transferring my "issues" onto her, and that she had done nothing but try to understand and engage with me in the hopes that I would truly know who she is and not pigeonhole her into the space of *"Entitled White Woman with Racist Friends."* Her last words to me were, *"Goodbye with love, I hope you grow as I will too."*

BAM! Door closed. I was blocked and deleted. I didn't get the chance to respond. I was right in the middle of typing my next response when I saw my name turn gray, which meant I was no longer part of the conversation. Boy, I wish I could have been a fly on the wall to see how the discussion ended. Based on what I witnessed, I'm sure the REAL problem was presumed to be me. Ha! I laughed out loud. None of the above was shocking to me. **Nine times out of ten, this type of conversation turns out this way with the Antagonist.**

I must also share that while Denise and I were having this conversation, Teresa was agreeing with everything I said. She was calling the other White women out left and right and very blatantly telling them they were making racist comments. She also told them that they **do** benefit from White Privilege, just like she does. **Very little attention was paid to her.** No one was getting angry with *her*. She was not accused of having a hidden agenda, nor was she accused of transferring her own issues onto the group of women engaging in this dialogue. She was not blocked and deleted. I will add that Denise was having other *lighthearted* conversations with the other White women in between her responses to me. She was having a good time with them, cyber laughing (LOL), asking when they were going to meet up for coffee, and engaging in other dismissive behaviors.

I'm not going to dissect this whole conversation. Instead, I want you to do so by asking yourself:

- *What do you see?*
- *What happened here?*
- *Do you think this dialogue was full of racist comments?*
- *If not, why not?*
- *How would you have responded in this situation?*
- *Would you have behaved like Denise?*
- *Would you have defended your friends?*
- *Would you call them out if you felt their comments were out of line?*
- *Do you agree with Denise?*
- *Do you disagree with Denise?*
- *Would you have blocked and deleted me?*
- *How would you have responded to my initial question?*

What I will say is that Denise is clearly the **epitome** of an **Antagonist**! And this is exactly how the Antagonist shows up in the women's empowerment arena. Sure, you'll encounter women like her in other spaces and places, but I want to shed glaring light on how these women use the New Age women's empowerment arena to hide their discomfort with race issues. **There are leaders, entrepreneurs, gurus, and many influential White women who proclaim they support and empower ALL women, yet they are clueless about, uninterested in, ill-quipped to, and/or afraid to discuss issues of race, culture, and ethnicity.** Now, before you get all fired up, I know this is NOT true of all White women. In the meantime, if the previously mentioned scenario and perspective bothers or angers you, you may have some Antagonist tendencies.

Denise is an Antagonist because she is clueless to the REAL race-related issues that women of color face every day, she is uninterested in learning from my experience as a Black woman, she is ill-equipped to deal with the emotions that arise in race talks, she's unwilling to see, hear, and acknowledge the truth of my Black experience, and she is in denial of her White Privilege.

You may be wondering what gives me the right to say such things. You may even think what I'm saying is "racist." And if so, **you are indeed an Antagonist.** Antagonists are good for using the term "reverse racism." Antagonists quickly dismiss the truths and realities of their women of color friends by asking questions or making statements like these:

- *"Don't you think you focus too much on race?"*
- *"Why does this have to be a race issue?"*
- *"I don't see race or color, I just see people."*
- *"It sounds like you (a person of color) have some personal issues with White people."*

And that's just the short list; see Chapter Five for more of these sorts of questions and statements and the uncomfortable truths that answer each one. So, what gives *me* the right to say such things? I'll tell you! Every single day of my life, I walk around, live, breathe, and navigate the world in this Black body of mine. And *every* single day, ever since Marty (my Antagonist from kindergarten) awakened me to the truth, I've experienced Antagonist after Antagonist, and I still do to this day. This is **my** truth whether you choose to believe it or not, and I know *for sure* this is the truth of many women of color and Black women.

You may be antagonizing women of color in your family, in your circles, on the job, on your social media— you may be antagonizing women of color *strangers*— and not even know it. Many of them won't have the courage to confront you, tell you how they feel, or that you've offended them, so I thought I'd help you out by sharing just a few ways the Antagonist thinks and behaves. How many of the following have you engaged in?

Ten Antagonistic Thoughts and Behaviors that Perpetuate White Privilege and Racism

1. Believing White Privilege doesn't exist.
2. Believing you do not benefit from White Privilege.
3. Believing or making the statement, "I don't see color, I see people."
4. Denying, minimizing, rationalizing, or justifying the racial experiences of people of color.
5. Comparing racism to other forms of oppression (such as sexism and classism).

6. Thinking and/or stating that a person of color is engaging in "reverse racism."

7. Becoming hurt, angry, and aggressive when the discussion of race comes up.

8. Failing to confront other White people when they make racist or privileged comments toward people of color.

9. Making a statement like this to a person of color: "Because I am poor, gay, or another type of marginalized person, I know how you feel."

10. Failing to hear and validate a person of color's racial experiences by defensively shifting the focus onto yourself, using questions or statements like:

   • *"Why are you making this about race?"*

   • *"You're pulling the race card."*

   • *"I'm a good person and I'm not racist."*

   • *"Well, that kind of stuff happens to me; are you sure it was racially motivated?"*

When you show up and engage with women of color and Black women in this way, you further antagonize them by adding extra weight to the oppression they already feel on a daily basis. Let me give you a few examples to help you understand this better.

Small acts can have tremendous impact! Take, for example, a mosquito bite. Being bitten by just one mosquito is enough to cause pain, and just one bite will drive you crazy with all the itching it brings on. Now imagine being bitten by twenty or thirty mosquitoes in a day, and now imagine receiving twenty or thirty mosquito bites every day of your life. Similarly, paper cuts, small and sometimes invisible, can cause severe, lingering pain. One is bad enough, but again, imagine getting twenty or thirty paper cuts all over your body in a day, and then the same amount or more every day *for the rest of your life.* **That's what happens when you show up and engage with Antagonistic thoughts and behaviors: you cause harm knowingly and unknowingly.** And finally, imagine if this pain is multiplied by three or four encounters with other Antagonists during just one day. Now we're talking about the pain of these *microaggressions* adding up to more than one hundred mosquito bites or paper cuts in *one* single day! Can you imagine the pain, discomfort, and agony you would experience? This is exactly what happens when you fail to acknowledge that White Privilege exists and that you benefit from it, when you don't see color, and/or when you continue to remain an Antagonist. And please do not take this lightly or make light of it because the impact is physically, emotionally, and spiritually tremendous and pervasive!

What if I told you I was fondled at the age of three months old and then sexually abused by an uncle at the age of seven, and then raped at the ages of fourteen, twenty-six, and thirty-one? What if I then went on to marry a man who was physically and verbally abusive, and he also forced me to have sex? What would you believe about me? What would you think about my situation? If you could speak to me about it, what would you say? Would you say or ask any of the following?

- *"Why didn't you get help?"*
- *"What did you do to cause the rape?"*
- *"Were you wearing provocative clothing?"*
- *"What kind of parents did you have to allow this to happen?"*
- *"Were you already having sex before you got raped at fourteen?"*

- *"If it happened once, why did you let it happen to you again?"*
- *"If you had that kind of childhood, why didn't you choose a better husband?"*
- *"Why are you staying with someone who beats you, yells at you, and forces you to have sex?"*
- *"There's no such thing as forced sex in marriage."*
- *"You must like being treated that way, because you stayed in the marriage."*
- *"What are you doing to keep attracting all this abuse into your life?"*

I certainly hope you would NOT think or ask any of the above, because if you did, you would be blaming the victim. You are blaming me. These are all called "victim-blaming statements and questions." As a trained and Certified Domestic Violence and Sexual Assault Advocate, I have heard these types of comments and questions from *"good and well-intentioned"* people who oftentimes just don't know any better. Before I became educated in this field, I too made many of those statements and asked those questions. But never again will you hear those or any variation of them come out of my mouth, because I know that by saying such things, I am further oppressing the recipient who is already feeling the weight of the oppression she is under. No, that is not my story, but what if it were? Victim blaming happens to survivors of sexual assault and domestic violence all the time, and it's painful, dismissive, and oppressive.

When you tell women of color and Black women that you don't believe White Privilege exists, you are essentially saying, *"I don't believe you experience racism from White people."* When you say you do not benefit from it, you deny the truth of a person of color's experience in which White Privilege in all its forms continues to oppress them. **When you say you don't see color, you are denying or minimizing the legacy of oppression faced by women of color and Black women, and you are failing to realize racism is something they may be facing on a daily basis.** When you make any of the ridiculous statements or comments I've shared so far, or the ones you'll hear about as you read farther in this book, you bite, cut, and revictimize your friend, your neighbor, your colleague, your family, your friends, and even strangers of color, Black women.

This is one of the most important points I want you to thoroughly digest from all this: **unintentional racism and oppression are just as wrong and painful as intentional racism and oppression are.** If you truly want to befriend, work with, and collaborate with women of color and Black women, you MUST be willing to examine what White Privilege truly is, how you benefit from it, and how you can begin to NOT further oppress the very women you want to align with. Today is the day you awaken to a new understanding, way of being, and way of engaging with women of color and Black women. **If you remain in denial of this TRUTH, your unintentional racism and oppression is now INTENTIONAL.** If you refuse to further examine your White Privilege and how it victimizes women of color and Black women, you show up in the world as an informed perpetrator, an Antagonist. Now you know better, so I hope you do better, because **ignorance is not bliss**; it's hurtful, oppressive, and lethal to the human spirit.

WAKE-UP CALL QUESTIONS

How many times have you shown up and behaved like Denise?

_____

_____

_____

_____

_____

How do you feel knowing that you've intentionally or
unintentionally revictimized your friends, colleagues, coworkers,
and family?

_____

_____

_____

_____

What keeps you from showing up like Teresa did?

_____

_____

_____

_____

Now that you know what an Antagonist is, how will you begin to transition to Advocate and eventually to Ally?

_____

_____

_____

_____

_____

_____

_____

Are you still denying any of these truths, and if so, why? What are you gaining from being in denial?

_____

_____

_____

_____

_____

_____

_____

_____

"We cannot educate White women and take them by the hand. Most of us are willing to help, but we can't do the White woman's homework for her. That's an energy drain."

GLORIA ANZALDÚA

Chapter 4

THE ADVOCATE

"I think it's very important for everyone in America to realize right now the state of our country, not just on this issue but on a lot of issues, that it is time to get active again. People have just sat back and just sort of said, oh, let somebody else do it for a long time, and we're seeing what's happening to the country, even freedom of speech. It's not going well. So I think this is a real opportunity for people to see, yes, if you do get out and you do get active, there are other people there. You just have to seek them out."

—*Mary Steenburgen*

Sometime in 2006, I started to build a "friendship" with a lovely White woman I worked with who I'll call "Gina." I admired her intentional efforts to challenge the workplace status quo, and I could sense she had some fire in her belly. She thought differently and seemed to care more deeply about social justice issues than many White women I knew. We began engaging in casual nonwork-related conversations about social justice, and eventually we dared to discuss daunting racial justice issues. The more we conversed, the more our friendship blossomed. I clearly remember sitting in her office one day when she said, *"Catrice, I have something to tell you."* I had no idea what she was going to say. Even though there was no reason for me to be fired, I wondered at first if that's what she was going to tell me. This thought came to mind because she seemed quite "chummy" with our boss, so maybe she had the inside scoop on that sort of information. The nervous look on her face, however, indicated that what she was about to reveal had nothing to do with me at all. With a slightly flushed face, Gina asked, *"Catrice, did you know that I am gay?"*

Honestly, I felt quite indifferent about her question because it really didn't matter to me one way or the other. My response to her was, *"No, I didn't know that, and I'm curious why you are telling me."*

She said, *"Well, I felt like our friendship was growing, and I just wanted you to know."*

I honored and respected her need to share this with me and simply said, *"Thanks for letting me know, but it doesn't matter."*

The ice was broken. Gina smiled. I sensed she was relieved to have spoken *her* truth. She had needed to get it off her chest. We were both comfortable with the conversation; in fact, I wondered if she had made this announcement to others in the past and maybe gotten a different response, possibly one of surprise and/or discomfort.

Over a period of several months, she began to share about her personal challenges in being a gay woman, and I shared about the challenges I faced not only as a Black woman, but also as a mother to a Black son. On one level we clicked, connected, and found a place of comfort in our conversations, and on another level, we'd soon find out it would require deeper trust, resiliency, and tenacity to truly develop a relationship that honored, valued, and supported our *unique* life experiences.

I discovered through our ongoing conversations that Gina was also an Advocate for racial justice issues. I must admit it was refreshing to be able to talk with a White woman who *got it,* or so I thought at the time. By "got it," I mean she listened without judgment, validated my race-related experiences, and did not revictimize me by doubting my reality and truth. I believed she was very sincere in her engagements. Several months passed, and we shared countless stories of social and racial injustices we experienced. We talked about just about everything, and not all our conversations were in total agreement. There were times when she could feel *only* the surface of what I was going through, and vice versa. We agreed that we'd be there for each other, that we'd serve as a reservoir for each other when one of us needed a safe place to rest and refuel our weary spirit. Speaking up about and fighting the injustices in the world is deep work that can drain you emotionally, and having a strong support system is essential. Without it, you may surely feel like giving up. We agreed to hang tight when the going got tough and rough. One of us would let go. One of us would fall down. But eventually, with the other's help, we'd get back up again.

I was beginning to think I had found a White Ally in the fight for racial justice. We worked at an organization with the mission statement of *"eliminating racism, empowering women."* So we were entrenched in social issues on and off the clock. We were both quite passionate about our work, which made our personal conversations easier to engage in. She would often talk about her frustration with people and systems that did not honor her marriage to another woman, and I'd talk about how I hated having to play a dual role in society as a Black woman, and how much fear I had for my Black son as he made the transition from boy to man, in a society where he was perpetually perceived as *"a feared and endangered species."*

But one day, Gina, who I had hoped was an Ally, showed up as an Advocate instead. I will *never* forget that moment. More than ten years later, I vividly remember it. During one of our typical conversations, I was quite passionate and borderline enraged about something that had happened to my son that caused me to fear for his life. I shared how one day walking home from school, he and his friends were harassed by some neighborhood kid. Long story short, my son was told to take off his new NFL football jersey and hand it over, or else. He did, and that moment changed our lives forever. I was furious about this incident. I was scared, pissed off, and terrified because he could have lost his life over a jersey. As I shared the incident with Gina, I cried and spoke with passionate concern, anger, and frustration. Not so much for this particular moment, but because I knew my son would experience countless moments like this *every day for the rest of his life.* She could hear my deep, aching pain. She knew I was both livid and frightened. She listened. She sat quietly on the phone. I continued to share with a sense of desperation. She continued to listen. And then, in the middle of one of my pauses, she said, *"Catrice, this is too heavy. I feel helpless. I don't know what to do. I don't feel like there is anything I can do. Please know that I love and appreciate you, but this is too much. I need a break."*

Disappointed. Angry. Hurt. My soul achingly screamed, *"How dare you walk out on me!"* That's what I wanted to say, but instead, I chuckled sarcastically and said, *"Okay, thanks for listening; I wish you well."* I believe that was the last time we spoke intimately on the phone. Ever. Although I was disheartened by her **need to escape,** I understood, and we remain *friendly* today. When I saw her at work the next day, I wasn't upset, and I didn't treat her any differently, nor did she have any hard feelings toward me. We continued to be friends; eventually, she got a job at a new company, and we still managed to keep in contact for a while. Occasionally, we would talk professionally about social justice issues going on in the community and the world, and here and there we'd talk about how our children were doing. Yeah... generally we engaged in *superficial* conversation. I didn't go there and respected her choice not to be taken there. She turned out to be an Advocate and not an Ally. I'll tell you why.

The Antagonist fights against race-related issues with defense mechanisms such as denial, minimization, justification, rationalization, and blame-shifting (in other words, they antagonize people of color), whereas an Advocate believes the experiences of those affected by racism and attempts to understand without blaming, persecuting, or revictimizing. The Advocate may not fully understand and own the comprehensiveness and pervasiveness of their White Privilege, but they acknowledge that it exists and that they benefit from it in some way. The Advocate seeks to understand without attacking, strives to learn instead of being in complete denial of their privilege, and works to become educated about their personal responsibility in ending racism and fostering inclusion. An Advocate stands alongside people of color and is genuinely interested in speaking up—and often does so—about social and racial injustices. Advocates are aware they must do their own personal work to use their White Privilege to end racism, but they are not always sure *exactly* what to do.

In my opinion, my friend Gina is an Advocate. Now, she might argue that she is an Ally, but let me tell you the difference. The United States of America has global allies who have committed to coming to the aid of the U.S. if a war breaks out. Even during calm times, these allies are strategically working to protect and defend the U.S, and they boldly step up during war and attacks on the U.S. They don't stop thinking about ways to protect the U.S., and there is never a moment they quit or give up, even when a situation becomes difficult. If they were to quit, they would no longer be allies and would instead move into the position of Advocate or Antagonist. My friend Gina showed up and spoke like an Ally. Over time, both in my presence and also when I wasn't around, she acted like an Ally. Yet in the case of our intimate conversations about race, racism, and the pain of oppression, she got tired. She couldn't take any more. It became too emotionally exhausting for her. She needed a break. She left me alone to fight this war by myself. She was NOT an Ally. At best, she is an Advocate. It's been over ten years since that moment, so maybe she has fully stepped into an Ally role. I don't know for sure. What I *do know* for sure is that **real allies** don't retreat during war; they fight until the battle is won.

You see, although there are ways that being a social and racial justice Advocate is a good thing, there are even more ways that it is detrimental. It's a neutral stance. People who are lukewarm, on the fence, gray, in the middle, or undecided are indifferent, confused, or afraid. They don't care one way or the other. They feel compelled to do something but are unsure of exactly what to do. They are afraid to make a choice. They *have* made a choice: to do enough to stay comfortable, or to do nothing at all. While this complacency provides the Advocate with tolerable comfort, deep within their soul there is unrest, a profound fear that keeps them paralyzed in indecision. Imagine a global war breaking out, and when it's time to fight, our allies remain seated in indecision. They have not suited up, loaded up, nor taken their battle positions, thus they have left *us* to fight alone. This is the mindset of the Advocate. They don't want to be seen and known as fighters. They don't want to leave the safe zone behind the White Picket Fence. They don't want to face and deal with the pain of loved ones hating or disowning them. They don't want to be categorized as a traitor or troublemaker. And the biggest truth of all is that they don't want to give up the very privileges they may deny they have.

To transition from an Antagonist to an Advocate requires a tremendous amount of personal sacrifice; after all, no one really wants to relinquish unearned privileges that have afforded them things they **did not** gain on their own merit. No one wants to admit and accept that many of the opportunities they've experienced did not happen solely because they were just great people. I mean, come on, who wants to accept the fact that they are farther along in life because of their skin color and not because of their personal accomplishments? If you happen to fall out with one of your friends or family members, it might be painful, but you can find a way to deal with it. But who in their right mind would want to intentionally alienate and cause strife within their relationships by standing up for truth and justice? It takes deep reflection, brutal honesty, and unwavering bravery to stand up and say, *"I didn't get to where I am and have what I do solely because of my own merit. White Privilege has granted me passes, opened doors, and provided opportunities that I did not earn."*

The war to end racism has lasted for centuries, and it may take many more centuries to finally win the battle. People have literally died, and so many are emotionally dying because of skin color. The fight is hard, emotionally taxing, spiritually draining, and sometimes physically debilitating. Women of color and Black women have been subtly or overwhelmingly experiencing these afflictions every day of their lives. So why would a White person, a

White woman like you, on top of all your other life challenges, get in line for this, say yes to it, and endure it? **Because if you don't, the war will *never* be won, and you'll be a contributor to the collateral damage.**

While it's appreciated, it's not enough to be an Advocate in the fight against racism and racial equality. You don't expect your friend who says they love and support you to be wishy-washy, especially during the times they need you most. Imagine your best friend telling you they will be with you and support you through some of the toughest times of your life, such as a divorce or the loss of a child, but they don't show up. They see you struggling. They see your pain. They hear your cries and shouts for help. They know you are in need of someone to stand in the gap with you, yet... they are too afraid to make the personal sacrifices to get off the fence and get in the trenches with you! **Advocates sometimes don't walk the talk.** They show up when they feel like it, when it's convenient, or when they know there won't be *significant* risk. Operating as an Advocate in the realm of social and racial justice work is a step in the right direction, but it's also **dangerous and can be counterproductive.**

As I mentioned in Chapter Three, there is a malady called *Racial Battle Fatigue*. Oh yes, and it's very real! For as long as I can remember, I've had a rebellious, warrior, stand-up-for-the-underdog mindset, and I have often used my voice to speak up about the injustices in the world. Even before I truly knew what prejudice, discrimination, and racism were, I always had a sense of when I or others were being treated differently or unfairly. I've been battling racism and discrimination all my life in one way or another, especially in my career and on the job. It never failed; at *every* job I've ever had, there was always some type of racial or cultural battle to be fought, and oftentimes, it was not my choice to get involved. There have been countless times where I would have rather closed my eyes and covered my ears to the intentional and unintentional racism I've seen, heard, and personally experienced in the workplace. And many times I did, just so I could survive another day and not be consumed by people's ignorance and hatred. It's hard! When I would ignore this type of behavior, *my soul wouldn't rest*, and when I'd call attention to it and address it, my soul would become weary. It was and is a constant battle of *"Should I say something, or just let this one roll off my back?"* Truthfully, this message, this book you are reading, has been a long time coming; it is a message developed over a lifetime. I finally reached the point where I had to not only share this message with the casual offender or colleague, but also to stand on a global platform and share it with the world. Let me tell you a few stories about my battlefield experiences.

In 1997, I took a position at a domestic violence and sexual assault shelter in my local community. Prior to this job, I was working "meaningless" jobs to make ends meet. I was presented with the opportunity to be an AmeriCorps volunteer, which essentially meant I was working a full-time job for a low monthly stipend. The pay was not enough to live on by any means, but I knew the opportunity would open future doors, so I said yes. My role was to basically do almost everything in the shelter, including answering the hotline, sorting donations, assisting with the children, going on advocate calls, being on call, counseling survivors, and everything in between. It was immediately obvious that most of the women who came to the shelter for refuge or services were White women. It was also obvious that ninety-seven percent of the staff were White women. And yes, I felt awkward and a little uncomfortable being in such an environment, because I knew what that meant for me as a woman of color, a Black woman. After I'd been there a while, the discussion I expected to take place finally did. The staff soon began to see me as the "spokesperson" for all women of color and Black women. A role I do not like playing, but if I need to, I will take it on. **A dreaded role that is tiring, frustrating, and emotionally depleting.**

Have you ever been asked to be the spokesperson for all White women, to be the voice for your race? I bet you either don't experience that *at all* or it happens only occasionally. By the way, that is another benefit of White Privilege: you don't have to be a spokesperson, because people of color are expected to already know and adapt to the ways of being White. We already know what it means to be a White woman, so you don't have to tell us or educate us. You don't have to be overwhelmed and exhausted with the expectation or obligation to stand up for White women, to educate others on what it means to be White, and/or to defend your race. Why? Because historically and still today, **being White is synonymous with being human.** So when you say, *"We're all human; why can't we just see and be people,"* you are essentially saying, *"Can't we all just be and act White,"* which of course is a **racist** statement, and you'll discover why.

So, back to this dreaded conversation. The Executive Director called me into her office one day and said, *"Catrice, as you can see, we are a very White organization, and we predominantly serve White women, but we want to employ more women of color and serve the women of color in our community. What would you suggest we do to improve our staff diversity and reach out to more women of color?"*

Want to know what my first thought was? Instantly, this response boiled up in my belly as it always does: *"Figure it out your damn self; I am **not** the spokesperson for women of color!"*

Why oh why do White women believe they can ask this

of women of color? I'll tell you why: *White Privilege.* White women have the belief that they can ask whatever they want of women of color, and they have the expectation that they will be answered. And if by chance a woman of color boldly calls them out by saying, *"I don't speak for all women of color,"* White women have **the nerve** to be hurt and offended. And to add insult to injury, when White women feel hurt and offended because a woman of color refuses to indulge or educate them, then they become angry and offensive, as if to say, *"You (woman of color) **owe me** this information; how **dare** you refuse me!"* White Privilege on top of White Privilege, and racial assault after racial assault; yeah, that's what it looks and feels like. This is the truth. This is what I've experienced too many times to count. This is my reality and the reality of many women of color and Black women. **If you're doing this, stop it and do your own work, which means figure it out your damn self!**

Flash forward in this story: because I wanted so desperately for women of color to come out of the shadows of shame, hurt, and pain, I agreed to help the organization reach out to and serve women of color. Of course this would not happen without heated discussions, White Privilege perspectives, unintentional racial assaults, defensiveness, frustration, and for me, *Racial Battle Fatigue!* Let me show you how seemingly small but powerful White Privilege is. After doing an informal assessment of the organization to include staffing patterns, training materials, policies and procedures, shelter rules, and the overall guidelines for being accepted into the shelter, I came to this conclusion: the organization wanted to reach out to women of color and serve them, yet the staff was ninety-seven percent White; they offered little to no training for the staff and crisis advocates on how domestic violence is different for women of color; the policies and procedures were not culturally sensitive; the shelter rules were created by and for White women; and the overall guidelines for being in the program weren't always conducive for women of color. *Why in the hell would women of color come there; feel wanted, safe, and secure; and/or stay there?* I knew if much of the status quo did not change, we would be setting women of color up to be revictimized, and they would return to their abusers.

There was no ethnic food in the refrigerator. The artwork did not portray women of color. There was no diversity in the selection of dolls for the little brown girls. There were no hair care products for Black women. Many of the materials were not translated into Spanish. If a woman of color were to arrive in the shelter, she'd likely be greeted by a White woman who did not understand her culture. A White woman who more than likely could not speak the client's first language. The woman of color would go upstairs to a refrigerator and pantry full of food that was not a usual part of her diet. Her daughters wouldn't have dollies that looked like them. Black women would not even be able to care for their unique hair, because there were no ethnic products available. The woman of color would walk around seeing White women running the show and plastered all over the walls. The direct and indirect messages she would receive would tell her, "I AM NOT WANTED HERE." And no matter what the staff said, the writing was on the wall. These women would NOT stay, and many of them didn't because of these **seemingly small-yet-powerful acts of White Privilege**. I knew I had my work cut out for me, and because my soul won't let me be silent or passively sit back and watch social and racial injustices occur, I rolled up my sleeves and went to work!

Significant and meaningful internal transformation happened during my two-year tenure at the shelter. I was eventually promoted to be the Community Education Coordinator and

Advocacy Trainer, which gave me the opportunity to make sure the staff and advocates got the diversity and cultural sensitivity training they needed, and I was able to be the voice out in the community, making sure OUR women got the services they needed with dignity and respect. This was a very fulfilling role and opportunity for me. It was this experience that set me on the path to becoming an advocate for women, a social and racial justice activist, a licensed and professional therapist, and the visionary of my own empowerment movement for women. **There were so many times I was physically exhausted and emotionally drained by standing up against racism, and for truth and justice for all, and there were so many times I wanted to quit, but my soul said otherwise.**

I was spiritually tired. I was fatigued. I experienced *Racial Battle Fatigue* yet again. Ironically, I suffered most at the hands of this group of predominantly White women who had signed on to "empower" ALL women, but either had no clue or no interest in making sure "all" included women of color and Black women. How can this be? When you White women say you empower ALL women, *do you really mean it?* Do you truly know what "empowering all women" entails, and are you sincerely and selflessly willing to do what it takes to walk your talk? Are you equipped to truly empower ALL women, to step outside your comfort zone? **If not, you're telling a lie.** And trust me, WE know it. Maybe you care and maybe you don't. **If you care, it's time to step up and become an Ally!** If you don't, it's *your* choice to continue to be an Antagonist who harms or an Advocate who is fickle, unreliable, and too selfish to *relentlessly* stand in the gap for ALL women.

The women I worked with at the shelter were certainly Advocates for women in several ways. However, many of them didn't realize how much of an Antagonist they were until it was brought to their attention (that's a benefit of White Privilege). There was ONE super-cool woman who *truly* was an Ally. I'll never forget the woman I'll call "Mary." *She got it.* She understood the best she could. She was supportive, insightful, careful, open, and deeply committed to doing HER racial justice work. I loved her! **I didn't have to explain, defend, teach, educate, or give away any of my precious mental, emotional, or spiritual energy.** We had many talks, and when I was tired, weary, and wanted to walk way, she was an Ally who offered the space for me to rest from the *Racial Battle Fatigue* by standing up and confronting White Privilege and her White colleagues **unapologetically**!

What a breath of fresh air! Just imagine what kind of organization the shelter could have been if more of the women were like Mary. Just imagine the impact in the community they could have had if there were more Marys working there. And most importantly, just imagine the lives that could have been saved, healed, and restored if more White women thought like, believed like, showed up like, and behaved like Mary. **Are you willing to be like Mary?** If you are a women's empowerment coach, speaker, community leader, or champion for women... you **MUST** be like Mary. *Advocacy is not enough!*

History repeated itself between 2006 and 2008. Again, I was soulfully led to work at another advocacy agency for women. I could just tell you the same story and end this chapter here, because the same things that had happened at the shelter happened at this advocacy agency in my current community. Same storyline. Same characters. Same plot. Same battle. Different women. After serving in the role of Advocacy Supervisor for less than a year, I was promoted to Racial Justice and Career Services Director. Interestingly, the advocacy agency's national slogan and mission statement includes the phrase, *"eliminating racism, empowering women."* I was so excited to work for an organization who so boldly proclaimed the urgency of addressing racism. I thought I would be able to talk openly about and actively engage in work around racism without it being taboo, or as many White women call it, *"Pulling out the race card."* I'd soon find out that the slogan was just some provocative words written on paper, at least for this local organization.

The Executive Director eventually asked me the same question I'd been asked at the shelter: *"Catrice, how do we .... Blah, blah, blah!"*

The thought that boiled up in my belly was basically the same as before, but it was a little different. This time, given the organization's mission and slogan, my thought was, *"What the hell are you guys doing up in here; you should already be doing the work to eliminate racism!"* But once again, I thought about the current and future women who needed this organization's services, and how the **potential for racial revictimization** was highly likely and pervasive. Once again, I rolled up my sleeves and went to work. This time would be the last time I sincerely, deeply, and intentionally did *this* kind of racial justice work.

Damn, I was tired! I just wanted to wake up in my Black body and go through life unbothered on my personal journey. Oh, but wait, that is not a luxury that women of color are automatically granted. That kind of life is **reserved for privileged White women.** Mind you, I never ever left the battlefield between 1997 and 2006, and frankly, I'm just too tired to tell you everything. Again, the work is not ever over, and I won't stop fighting until I take my last breath.

Just like the shelter, the advocacy agency was mostly White women, with very similar perspectives and practices. There were other organizations in the community doing outreach, advocacy, and education around diversity and cultural sensitivity. However, no one was aggressively tackling racism. It made sense to me that if our goal was to eliminate racism, then we had better do it intentionally and relentlessly. I suggested to the Executive Director that we do something strikingly different by tackling racism at the root, plucking it at its core, and addressing the reality and pervasiveness of White Privilege. With a little hesitation, she agreed. I created a proposal, plan, and strategy; they were approved; and hell was about to break loose, and it did. You see, cultural sensitivity training and diversity workshops address only the *symptoms* of racism. Addressing White Privilege and the deep, systemic roots of White Supremacy and racism are absolute musts for the **evil system** to be dismantled. There is no better way, no matter how hard and exhausting it is.

I started conducting trainings and workshops, networking and collaborating with other activists, and I realized **WE had to walk our talk**, we had to pluck our racism roots from within. The staff was informed they would have to participate in White Privilege 101 training, and at first, many were confused, but most were on board—or so they thought. The year prior, when I served as the Advocacy Supervisor, *everyone* "loved" me! I was so smart, savvy, charismatic, optimistic, supportive, and brilliant, and I was deemed a significant asset to the company, especially because I turned that department around on a dime and in no time. The advocates were excelling like they never had before. This was one of the reasons I got the promotion over other staff who had been there longer than I had. Catrice was a *shining star!* Until... I passionately and consistently spoke truth and brought the dark into the light. "Women empowering women" quickly turned into her versus us. I suited up, I put on my battle armor, and I stood my ground despite the circumstances.

The White Privilege 101 internal training began. To summarize, tempers flared, attitudes were evoked, aggressions emerged, and essentially, only about a quarter of the staff were even remotely interested in learning about White Privilege and how it perpetuates racism. It didn't matter how I served it up; **they were not hungry and refused to eat**. While my Executive Director was very pleased with the format and presentation style, most of my colleagues were not having it! Ninety-five percent of them became offended, hurt, and defensive, and some were outright aggressive, but most of them were passive-aggressively pissed off! Catrice, the shining star, eventually became the *pot-stirrer*, the *race-card puller*, the *troublemaker*, the target of the very White Privilege and racism they **supposedly stood against**, and the staff person who went from receiving cheers and applause to getting the cold shoulder and silent treatment. **Talk about revictimization!**

How could this be true in an organization with a mission statement that included *"eliminating racism, empowering women"*? How could this organization be fighting against racism to solely preserve... White Privilege! **This is the perfect example of the danger and lethality of being an Advocate.** This was an advocacy agency, straddling the fence, standing in the middle, and unwilling to take the risk and to sacrifice "self" to do the hard work of racial justice. This was a perfect example of how reckless it is to say YOU empower ALL women when you *really* don't. This is a perfect example of someone talking the talk but *afraid to walk the walk*. This is a perfect example of how White Privilege, when left unaddressed and not aggressively plucked from its devastating roots, will continue to hurt, harm, offend, wound, and break down the mental, emotional, and physical natures of women of color and Black women. Honestly, to put it bluntly... this organization, at this particular time, **was living a lie!** You might be living a lie too, especially if you proclaim that you empower all women, whether in your work or personal life, if you are **not** willing to or capable of doing so.

Needless to say, *Racial Battle Fatigue* continued for me. It became too much to bear alone. I started missing days at work due to irritable bowel syndrome. The emotional weight was too heavy. I didn't have any Allies, and my colleagues of color were tired of fighting too. You see, White Advocates can choose to pack up and leave the battlefield any time they want, and never look back, return, or feel guilty about their departure. In fact, many of them feel liberated from the struggle. Women of color and Black women stay on the battlefield *all day every day.* Sometimes we retreat to the bunker because we need to catch our breath, heal, and regain our strength, and other times we fight until we are dead tired. For me, it showed up in the forms of cold sores and irritable bowel syndrome. **We don't get a break!** We can't just walk away, and when we do, like I did when I finally resigned from the advocacy agency, the bombs are still being dropped. We still duck and dodge. We try to ignore or avoid them, but when your soul is an activist for social and racial justice, you suit up and take your place on the field again.

In 2008, I left the workforce for good and started my own company. This way I knew I wouldn't have to deal with the daily workplace racial drama anymore, and while that is true, I will never ever escape it completely while living in this Black skin.

Here are some questions for you to consider as a White woman:

- *On how many jobs have you had to fight a racial fight?*

- *How often in life are you fatigued because you are on the battlefield for racial justice?*

- *How many times in a day are you defending and standing up for the White race?*

- *How many Black or brown friends and colleagues have you lost due to them not understanding your racial struggle and pain?*

I conclude your answers are "never" or "rarely," and the reason is **because you don't have to**; that's how you benefit from White Privilege. You know nothing about *Racial Battle Fatigue*, so don't pretend like you do, and **stop** revictimizing women of color and Black women who are *damn tired* of trying to get you to understand their pain and struggles. **Just listen and validate their experiences! They are NOT crazy, so please stop denying their truths.**

For the past seven years as an entrepreneur, White Privilege and racism have shown up differently for me. I've avoided this message for seven years, and actually for a lifetime. Yet it won't leave me alone, because I know there are women of color and Black women who are suffering due to intentional and unintentional racism and White Privilege. I finally said yes to my soul's calling. Again, I've rolled up my sleeves, and I'm ready to work **by any means necessary**. As Joan of Arc said, *"I am not afraid; I was born for this."* And so it begins. I am ready to do this work alone if I have to, but I hope **you will choose** to suit up and join me, to lay down your Antagonistic weapons, get off the dangerous fence of Advocacy, and become a relentless Ally, so that ALL women will be empowered to live a free and unburdened life, and to simply just BE.

WAKE-UP CALL QUESTIONS

How have you been showing up as an Advocate for women of color and Black women, and what kind of collateral damage has that caused?

_____

_____

_____

_____

_____

As a friend, coworker, colleague, coach, teacher, or leader, how will you begin to acknowledge the Racial Battle Fatigue experienced by the women of color and Black Women you know? And how will you choose to NOT add to it?

_____

_____

_____

_____

_____

_____

_____

What are you willing to lose or sacrifice to get off the fence of Advocacy to become an Ally for women of color and Black women?

_____

_____

_____

_____

_____

_____

_____

_____

_____

_____

_____

_____

_____

_____

_____

_____

_____

_____

_____

Chapter 5

THE WHITE PRIVILEGED WOMAN

"Fellow White Feminist, it's time for us to
take a damn seat and listen."

—*Shelby Knoxx, Feminist Organizer and Revolutionary*

If this chapter's title and opening quote offend you, piss you off, or turn you off, you *are* an Antagonist. If you thought of defending yourself against these truths, you are an Antagonist. If you want to slam this damn book shut right now, you are indeed an Antagonist. One of the most telling signs that you are a *social and racial justice* Antagonist is the immediate feeling of anger and defensiveness that rises and begins to boil over in your belly. Next is a quick surge of fear that's disguised by an audacious spiel of the same old *tired* responses to racism. Responses that Black women have heard so many countless times before that they know what the Antagonist will say before she says it. Let me prove this truth.

If you are a White woman in today's world, you are the most privileged woman that has ever existed. You are the *perceived* epitome of beauty. You are the standard of what it means to **be** a woman. You have benefited and continue to benefit from the *unearned* privilege of having White skin. When you get too frustrated, or too tired of talking about and/or dealing with race issues, you can say *"I've had enough of this,"* and you can walk away and ignore the topic. I'm sure you've done so at least once in your lifetime.

How did you feel while reading the previous paragraphs? What thoughts came to mind and what statements did you make? Perhaps you thought or said one of the following highly aggressive and antagonistic statements:

- *"This is some bullshit right here!"*
- *"Catrice, isn't what you are saying 'reverse racism'?"*
- *"Why is this even an issue? I don't see race or color; I just see people."*
- *"White Privilege—I've never heard of it before."*
- *"You don't know me personally, so you can't lump me in with all other White women."*
- *"Really. I don't believe this is true, nor have I ever thought about this."*
- *"I didn't grow up with a silver spoon in my mouth."*
- *"There's no way I'm privileged. I came from a family where I had to work hard for everything I got."*
- *"Catrice, you obviously have some personal issues you are trying to project onto me."*
- *"Sounds like you are angry at one White person and taking it out on me."*
- *"You don't know my story; I am far from privileged."*
- *"I'm so tired of hearing about racism."*
- *"I've been bullied, teased, harassed, and picked on my whole life, so I understand."*
- *"If I don't want to talk about racism, I don't have to."*

- *"I grew up poor and am not privileged."*
- *"I actively work to end the pain of racism, so I'm not privileged."*
- *"I'm lesbian or gay, so I understand the struggle and pain of discrimination."*
- *"Who the hell are you to sit on your high horse and tell me I am privileged?"*
- *"I don't get it. I don't understand. What do you mean I am privileged?"*
- *"Catrice, you are the one who is racist!"*

I could write fifty or more responses, but this should suffice. Nine times out of ten, you thought or said one of these statements exactly. How do I know? Because this is the **racially unique** but overindulged-in language of White Privilege that has been passed down from generation to generation. This luxury of not knowing, not having to know, and/or not *wanting* to know what White Privilege is and how you benefit from it is the biggest slice of the privilege pie that you gobble up and digest every living, breathing day of your life. Now, perhaps you didn't think or say *any* of those things at all, and if that's true, I'm delighted! I'm delighted because it's an indication of your willingness to see, exist, and live beyond the *White Picket Privileged Fence* that your forefathers, foremothers, and White society have purposely and systematically built for you. If you feel offended, confused, hurt, or pissed off by what's been stated in this chapter, my theory is well under way to being proven. But quite honestly, my goal is NOT really to "prove" anything to you. As I said before, you can shut this book right now and go on with your life, or you can tighten up your seat belt and hold on for this awakening-your-consciousness ride.

My intention for this book is to start and engage in conversations that *wake people up* to uncomfortable truths and painful-but-authentic realities. My intention is that this book will lead to honest dialogues about women, race, and gender. My intention is to offer you a new perspective, a new lens through which you can see the world and the people around you with awakened, curious, and honoring eyes. My intention is that you will become more conscious about the power you have to create real, transformational social and racial justice change. And finally, my intention is to close the debilitating division between women worldwide by honoring and valuing our differences, so we can create the **undisputed** unity necessary for us to truly save and change the world. Not one of my intentions will produce fruit unless THIS conversation, the one you and I are engaging in right now, happens repeatedly, truthfully, and consistently... until we take our last breaths.

So let's explore the uncomfortable truth that has been shared in these pages. White Privilege is real! People of color have NOT made this up. **They are not delusional!** They are not crazy. They are not exaggerating their reality. They are not taking their personal frustrations out on you, and last but most importantly, women of color and Black women are NOT racist for suggesting, believing in, and pointing out White Privilege. And here's a bonus nugget: **every time you believe, suggest, or speak out loud any of the aforementioned untruths, you antagonize, wound, revictimize, and oppress women of color and Black women.** Every White woman, regardless of age, sexual preference, gender identity, faith, religion, geographic location, socioeconomic status, or any other personal characteristic is a woman of racial privilege. Period!

Now I'm going to elaborate on this more throughout the book, but if you don't believe White Privilege is true, one of two things will happen. You will either continue to be in denial and be destructive, demeaning, and oppressive to the very women of color and Black women that you say you honor, value, and appreciate by not doing your own homework and personal work to eradicate racism. Or you will say, *"Hmm, what if White Privilege is true?"* and you will do your homework and your personal work, and stop the gushing and infectious wound of racism from bleeding all over the world and seeping into future generations. Take your pick. The choice is yours. **Ignorance is not bliss.** *Ignorance is toxic, perpetual, dangerous, and lethal.* I suggest you do your homework and personal work to avoid inflicting pain on other human beings who **did not** choose the color of their skin.

In the Introduction to this book, I mentioned that White Privilege is a detriment to you too. When you truly see it, believe it, and own, it you'll understand why. It's true that I can't make you believe anything I say, but I will offer you this: **while your White Privilege affords you countless benefits, it equally burdens you with some harsh realities.** Your privilege is under attack. It's being rightfully dismantled right before your eyes, and while you can't quite see it, put your finger on it, and/or understand it, the White Picket Fence is falling piece by piece. People of color have said "no more," and White people are feeling the rebellion and uprising like never before. While Privilege is under siege, and many White people feel threatened. As racial and ethnic demographics steadily change in the United States and the world, the power of White Privilege becomes weak and diluted.

As the *browning of America* continues, the physical presence of "White" or "White-looking" people dramatically decreases. Now you may not see yourself as privileged, racist, superior, and/or a member of the Ku Klux Klan (KKK) or any other White Supremacy group, but those who do are feeling mighty threatened right now and are enraged about this "browning." Like it or not, believe it or not, Dylan Roof, the Charleston, South Carolina racist killer, felt threatened and enraged. In fact, before horrifically shooting nine innocent Black church members, he stated, *"You're raping our women and you have to go."* You can read up on Dylan if you're so inclined; however, one point is very clear: Dylan felt threatened by the dwindling of White Power and White Privilege, and he took it upon himself to ignite a "race war," as he called it.

Dylan Roof is NOT the only White person who feels threatened, and all the social uprisings happening in the world illustrate this fear of loss of power. When you are the *perceived* "majority" who has been comfortable being powerful and in power, and enjoy being the dominant "norm," if you will, anything or anyone who threatens your social status becomes a threat, the enemy. Your sense of identity is being challenged and your power is being pulled from your hands. Truth is, White Privilege is turning into *White Fragility*, a term coined by Robin DiAngelo to describe the defensive behaviors White people engage in (such as crying, anger, and withdrawal) when they experience what they consider to be "too much" racial stress. White Fragility is another way those who hold White Privilege can oppress people of color. **Whether you know it or not, White Privilege is a detriment to the mental and emotional well-being of those who hold it.** The more intentional research and personal work you do around this privilege, the more you'll realize for yourself exactly how detrimental it is.

All right, it's time to shift into another level of understanding. Tighten up your seat belt! Let's dig deeper into the uncomfortable truths around White Privilege. Let's look again at the thoughts and statements you might have had in response to the notion of White Privilege, and this time I'll counter each one with an uncomfortable truth that shows how the original statement exemplifies and/or perpetuates White Privilege and racism.

THOUGHT OR STATEMENT	UNCOMFORTABLE TRUTH
"This is some bullshit right here!"	No, it's the truth, and the truth will first piss you off and then set you free.
"Catrice, isn't what you are saying 'reverse racism'?"	There is no such thing as reverse racism. This is a cop-out response used to shift the focus of your own privilege and racist tendencies. Racism = power + privilege, and people of color collectively do not have power or privilege.
"Why is this an issue? I don't see race or color, I just see people."	Being Colorblind is a lazy, dangerous excuse to avoid heated discussions about race, to maintain your denial of privilege, and to give you a false sense of not being racist.
"White Privilege—I've never heard of it before."	Ignorance is not bliss; it's dangerous and lethal. Ignorance perpetuates privilege and racism in both intentional and unintentional ways.

THOUGHT OR STATEMENT	UNCOMFORTABLE TRUTH
"You don't know me personally so you can't lump me in with all other White women."	It doesn't matter. Regardless of age, sexual preference, gender identity, faith, religion, geographic location, socioeconomic status, class, and any other personal characteristic, all White people have White Privilege.
"Really. I don't believe this is true, nor have I ever thought about this."	It is true. You can't see oxygen with the naked eye, but you breathe it in every day and benefit from it. Your lack of thinking about it and owning it contributes to the collateral damage of racism.
"I didn't grow up with a silver spoon in my mouth."	You can change your economic, wealth, and class status but not the color of your skin. There is no comparison, so retire that one.
"There's no way I'm privileged. I came from a family where I had to work hard for everything I got."	Hard work doesn't make you exempt from privilege. Look how hard Black slaves worked for centuries. It didn't stop the racism and oppression they endured.

THOUGHT OR STATEMENT	UNCOMFORTABLE TRUTH
"Catrice, you obviously have some personal issues you are trying to project onto me."	No. This is your White Fragility showing up, which is another form of privilege where White people expect people of color to talk nicely to them about privilege, race, and racism.
"Sounds like you are angry at one White person and taking it out on me."	See ALL of the above.
"You don't know my story; I am far from privileged."	I do know your story. No matter what you've encountered in your life, you've been shielded from racism due to your White Privilege.
"I'm so tired of hearing about racism."	Great. Then do something to eradicate it, and if you're tired of hearing and talking about racism, multiply that by infinity, because that's how tired people of color are from experiencing it. Denying your White Privilege contributes to the continuation of racism.

THOUGHT OR STATEMENT	UNCOMFORTABLE TRUTH
"I've been bullied, teased, harassed, and picked on my whole life, so I understand."	It's unfortunate that you've experienced such treatment, and I hope you were eventually able to escape it. However, people of color can never escape the color of their skin, so they will be discriminated against until they take their last breath.
"If I don't want to talk about racism, I don't have to."	You're right. One of the biggest perks of White Privilege is to NOT have to talk about race and racism. Silence is agreement, and it's toxic.
"I grew up poor and am not privileged."	You can escape poverty if you choose; however, you cannot escape the color of your skin. Stop using this countertactic. It's tired, and it perpetuates racism.
"I'm lesbian or gay, so I understand the struggle and pain of discrimination."	Certainly being lesbian or gay brings many challenges, but you can "hide" your preference if you choose. People of color do NOT have this option. Stop saying this; it is offensive.

THOUGHT OR STATEMENT	UNCOMFORTABLE TRUTH
"Who the hell are you to sit on your high horse and tell me I am privileged?"	Who am I? I am a Black woman who cannot escape her skin; who has dealt with a lifetime of discrimination, prejudice, and racism just for living while Black; and who has experienced more of this from White women than from any other human being on the planet.
"I don't get it. I don't understand. What do you mean I am privileged?"	Ignorance is no excuse. Step outside of your White Picket Fence and do your research on White Privilege, and then do your own personal work.
"Catrice, you are the one who is racist!"	Racism = power + privilege. Socially and systemically, I do NOT have either power or privilege. Next to the White man, White women are the second most privileged people in the world. Educate yourself.

I'm sure you have a lot of questions popping up in your head right now. The one question I want you to call forth is, *"What if ALL this is true?"* And then think about how your unknowing, lack of consciousness, and unintentional acts have directly and indirectly impacted the lives of women of color and Black women. **Now, you can continue to argue that there is no truth to what I've shared so far, and that's fine, but know this: your doing so is like carbon monoxide—invisible, real, and deadly.** This is the mindset of a passive-aggressive Antagonist. Unintentional harm due to lack of knowledge is no less painful and oppressive than blatant racial attacks, and you must awaken to the truth that carbon monoxide kills even though you can't see it or touch it.

Picture this: you arrive at a friend's house, and you immediately notice that she looks tired, sick, and beat down. Your friend is obviously suffering from something. She tells you there's something in the air making her sick. You look around, but you can't see anything or smell anything. But you really want to *believe* and help her. You watch her become more and more lethargic and unresponsive as time goes by. She continues to ask for your help and keeps saying there's something in the air. Suddenly, she falls to the floor and her life begins to slip away. Will you continue to stand there and say you don't see or smell anything toxic in the air, or will you *believe* your friend's reality and intervene right away? I believe I know the answer to that, and so do you.

I get it. I understand that believing, accepting, and owning that you were born with invisible, **unearned** privileges based on your skin color may be a hard truth to swallow. Having me and the world tell you that you're a White Privileged woman may cause you to feel confused or angry. But just like the carbon monoxide example, you don't have to see or touch your privilege for it to be REAL. I'm not going to go into a long educational process to make my point. Again, this is *your* work to do, and you must do it.

Like your friend in the story above, women of color and Black women need you to believe them and take action immediately! They KNOW there is something in the air that strangles the life out of them, and they are tired of trying to convince White people that your White Privilege toxically threatens their livelihood. If you are a true and relentless Antagonist, you're probably thinking, *"I don't believe this bullshit; I am NOT privileged!"* If you are an Advocate, you are on the fence; you're finding it hard to believe, but you are curious enough to explore it and begin doing your own work. If you are a White Ally, you're in agreement, and you are already not only doing *your* work, but are also in the trenches with women of color fighting against racism and challenging your White friends by unapologetically calling them out on their racist behaviors.

This is your WAKE-UP CALL and an open invitation to experience an *Awakened Conscious Shift*. A dramatic shift, and maybe even a sobering reality check about life outside the White Picket Fence is necessary for you to move from Antagonist to Advocate, and eventually to Ally. You see, I can share my experiences, my realities, and my truths until my face turns blue, and believe me there have been moments when it's felt like that was happening during race discussions. I can attempt to educate you in hopes that one day the light bulb will go on for you and you'll finally say, *"I get it."*

Can you imagine how much time, effort, and soul energy that takes? It's tiring, it's exhausting, it's downright frustrating, and although I will *never* give up the fight against racism, I will choose my battles wisely. My work is to share my experience and my truth about privilege and racism; your work is to hear what I express and make a choice to ignore it or do something about it. **The real NAKED truth is that racism is NOT a person of color's problem to solve. Racism was created, indoctrinated, upheld, and continues to be perpetuated by White people; therefore, it is White people's problem to solve.** We people of color, the recipients of racism, must fight against it and work to eliminate it, but we cannot do it alone. You must do your part. **You must do your work!**

If by chance you are interested in learning more about your White Privilege, there is a plethora of resources, articles, and books available to you. Peggy McIntosh, a pioneer in the White Ally movement, describes White Privilege as, *"...an invisible package of unearned assets that I can count on cashing in each day, but about which I was 'meant' to remain oblivious. White privilege is like an invisible weightless knapsack of special provisions, maps, passports, codebooks, visas, clothes, tools, and blank checks."* I will add to this. All these perks, passes, and advantages have been given and not earned, and they allow you and those with White skin to enter places people of color can't, receive special treatment people of color are not offered, and gain access to opportunities that people of color can't leverage.

If you don't know who Peggy McIntosh is, today is the day you meet her and listen to what she has to say. That is your homework. You can choose to hear what she has to say, or you can choose to go back behind the White Picket Fence and continue to intentionally and unintentionally **assault and oppress** women of color and Black women. The choice is yours. I suggest you Google and read Peggy's article, "White Privilege: Unpacking the Invisible Knapsack." It's a start.

All human beings need to become more conscious and awakened to the truths and realities that people who are different from them are experiencing. You'll find many community and social leaders who say, *"Let's not focus on the differences,"* but I believe it's our differences that make us uniquely diverse. We need to see our differences so we can respect them, appreciate them, value them, and honor them; so we can *truly* see another person's personal experiences. Wake up to this reality:

- *Men have privileges that women do not.*
- *The rich have privileges that the poor do not.*
- *Heterosexuals have privileges that gay people do not.*
- *Christians in America have privileges that non-Christians do not.*
- *Thus, White people have privileges that people of color do not.*

You cannot believe some privileges exist and deny others. If you are willing to admit you have White Privilege and want to become an Ally in the fight to end racism, **you must stop the hypocrisy!** You cannot say you fight for and stand with all women, yet refuse to admit that you have been given unearned power and privilege over women of color. **Stop it. It's a lie, and we *know* the truth.** If you want to say truthfully that you empower all women, you must also be courageous enough to say that you are a White Privileged woman, one who is actively standing with brown and Black women in the fight to eliminate racism.

You must be willing to use your power and privilege to stand in the gap and be an Ally who walks the talk. **Anything less**

than that is hypocrisy and means you are an Antagonist.
While you may believe you are hiding your hypocrisy behind the
shield of this exclusive New Age feminist movement and getting
away with it, awakened and conscious women of all shades see
you as a liar. You know better, you are better, and in the words of
Maya Angelou, *"Do the best you can. Then when you know better,
do better."* And lastly, I agree with Shelby Knoxx's statement
wholeheartedly: *"Fellow White Feminist, it's time for us to take a
damn seat and listen."*

Want to know what you can do **right now** to really hear
what I am saying and to begin to dismantle the real, pervasive,
oppressive systems of White Privilege and racism? Racism is not
always loud, boisterous, aggressive, and blatant. Most racism is
invisible, silent, passive, and unintentional, but it's just as painful,
disrespectful, and oppressive. Here's how to begin your work:

- *Please stop defining racism as overt hatred expressed
  only by "bad" people, and instead start seeing the silent,
  often covert racism of White privilege (held by all White
  and White-appearing people) that women of color and
  Black women see and experience.*

- *Please stop priding yourself on being Colorblind. Please
  stop bringing up what women of color and Black women
  are doing to themselves, and instead start asking what
  you are doing to contribute to it.*

- *Please stop wondering why women of color and Black
  women keep talking about race, and instead start asking
  yourself how you benefit from being White and why you
  are NOT talking about race.*

- *Please stop getting defensive when women of color and
  Black women express their frustrations about racism and*

oppression, and instead start asking yourself why you are not frustrated and angry about being White.

- *Please stop feeling hurt and wounded when women of color and Black women point out your White Privilege, and instead start owning your Whiteness and how you benefit from it.*

- *Please stop pushing away, ignoring, deleting, and blocking women of color and Black women when they openly engage in direct race dialogues, and instead start asking yourself why you are running away.*

- *Please stop believing that because you have Black friends and/or are married to a Black man that you are exempt from White Privilege and racism, and instead start understanding that racism is systemic and the United States of America was built with racist bricks and mortar.*

- *Please stop pointing out the negative portrayal of "Blackness" on television and in the media, and instead start paying attention to the buffet of White Supremacy you are served on every media platform 24/7.*

- *Please stop expecting women of color and Black women to **watch their tone** when they speak to you about your privilege, and instead start asking yourself why you expect them to protect your White Fragility.*

- *Please stop writing off the pain of women of color and Black women because they speak so passionately about their struggles, and instead start wondering why you **do not** have to speak so passionately about the pain of being White.*

- *Please stop proclaiming that you are **NOT** racist, and instead start understanding how you benefit from racism.*

- *Please stop expecting women of color and Black women to trust you because you're White, and instead start considering the various reasons why they should **not** trust you because you ARE White.*

- *Please stop asking or expecting women of color and Black women to pull you to the side to talk to you about privilege and racism, and instead start being open to hearing about it on the spot. Oppression doesn't pause for us; therefore, we will no longer pause for the oppressor.*

- *Please stop expecting and demanding that women of color and Black women make you feel safe and comfortable during "race talks," and instead start understanding that they don't have the privilege of feeling safe when racism is attacking them every day.*

- *Please stop biting your tongue and ignoring the racist comments and behaviors of your White friends, colleagues, and family members, and instead start realizing that your silence means you agree with them, and it perpetuates racism.*

- *Please stop saying, **"I am not my ancestors; I didn't own slaves,"** and instead start accepting that racism exists as an institutional system and say, **"What can I do personally to dismantle it?"***

- *Please stop saying to women of color and Black women that because you are lesbian or gay, you know what it feels like to be discriminated against, and instead start understanding that it is not the same and never will be until racism dies.*

- *Please stop saying you are my "sistah," and instead start accepting that you have no idea of the struggles of "sistahs." This is Misappropriation of Culture.*

- *Please stop misappropriating and stealing our culture at your convenience, and instead start realizing that we do not have the privilege of using or abusing our culture to get what we want, sound cool, and then throw it back when it's no longer advantageous to us.*

- *Please stop expecting or asking women of color and Black women to explain, justify, or educate you on issues related to diversity, cultural sensitivity, privilege, and racism, and instead start accepting that it is **your** work to do, and in fact, **it is** racial aggression to make such requests.*

- *Please stop asking Black women if you can touch their hair, and stop bombarding them with a thousand rude questions about how they did it, how much it cost, did it hurt, and instead start asking yourself why you think it's okay to ask these and other ridiculously offensive questions about our ethnic identity.*

- *Please stop telling women of color and Black women to just **"get over it"** or saying we live in a **"post-racial America,"** and instead start realizing we will get over it when White people stop oppressing us, and even that will not signify a post-racial America.*

- *Please stop saying you're a feminist if you are unwilling to accept your White Privilege, and instead start accepting that if you don't believe you are further oppressing women of color and Black women by remaining in denial of this truth, **then you are living a big fat LIE!***

Denial is deadly! When you deny your White Privilege, you deny the stories, truths, and realities of women of color and Black women. Denial keeps you Colorblind, which keeps you unconscious of the real struggles of your Black and brown sisters.

Denial affords you the luxury of shielding yourself from the harsh realities that women of color face every day of their lives. **Denial helps you actively participate in the perpetuation of racism whether you mean to or not.** Instead of continuing to deny your White Privilege, maybe you'll take Shelby Knoxx's advice: *"Fellow White Feminist, it's time for us to take a damn seat and listen."*

WAKE-UP CALL QUESTIONS

How has the denial of your White Privilege been a detriment to you and the women of color you've engaged with?

_____

_____

_____

_____

So, how many paper cuts have you given to women of color and Black women in your lifetime?

_____

_____

_____

_____

How has the denial of your White Privilege been a detriment to you and the women of color you've engaged with?

_____

_____

_____

_____

Can you count the number of times you've unintentionally offended, hurt, oppressed, and/or silenced women of color and Black women with the infliction of microaggressions? How do you feel now that you know the pain you've caused?

_____

_____

_____

_____

_____

_____

_____

Now that you know better, how will you do better?

_____

_____

_____

_____

_____

_____

_____

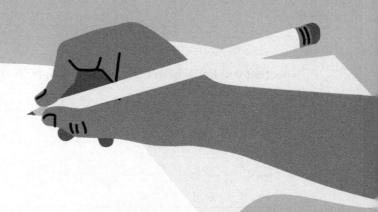

Chapter 6

INTERSECTIONALITY

The Crossroads Between Race & Gender

"What better reason to risk your own freedom than to fight for the freedom of others?"

—*Brittany "Bree" Newsome*

If I asked you what it meant to be White and female, what would you say? If I asked you what it means to be a White woman in the world, how would you respond? What situations, circumstances, challenges, and/or issues are unique to being a White woman? Not a woman in general, but a White woman specifically? Have White women endured anything in particular because of their Whiteness? Do White women have distinct challenges they face *every* day? As you search for the answers, remember that I'm not talking about women's equality, the suffrage movement, abortion, sexual abuse, rape, domestic violence, sexism, workplace harassment, pay inequality, or other challenges and difficulties that all women may face, but those situations that are *specifically unique* to White women. So... what did you come up with? What's your response when you are asked, *"What is it like to be White and female in the world?"*

I could be wrong, but I'm going to guess you struggled to pinpoint any specific problems, challenges, issues, difficulties, or barriers that you face as a result of being a female with White skin. It's true that you may have been able to identify some issues related to your ethnicity, such as being Dutch, Swedish, German, Italian, and/or Irish. But even then, especially in America, I bet you don't feel the oppression of "being" that ethnicity on a daily basis. Why? Because many White people have relinquished their ethnicity and now identify only as "White." If you did come up with an issue due to your ethnicity, it might be easy for you to stop identifying with your ethnicity to minimize or eliminate those challenges. In other words, if you never told anyone what your ethnicity is, I bet those "ethnic-specific" challenges you came up with would no longer occur.

I rarely hear White people identify themselves as Irish American or German American (although I do hear people identifying as Italian American more often). Why is this? Why do most "White" people not identify themselves according to their heritage and ethnicity? **Because being White in this world is the ultimate privilege that allows you the luxury of not having to discover, explain, know, or care what it means to be White. Being White is synonymous with being human.** Have you ever said, *"We're all just human; we all matter"*? Yeah, that insulting statement made to women of color and Black women translates into, *"To be human is to be White; why don't you just be human and everything will be okay."* Uh oh! Your reckless comment just caused a crash at the intersection of life for women of color. **And it's too late; the collateral damage has been done.**

The intersection I'm talking about is called *"Intersectionality."* Let's define "Intersectionality," a term coined by Kimberlé

Crenshaw. Kimberlé is a scholar, professor, and activist who specializes in race and gender issues. She's published articles on civil rights, Black feminist legal theory, and racism and the law. Intersectionality wasn't new when Kimberlé introduced it to feminist theory in the 1980s, but it didn't gain popularity until she began shining the light on this critical intersection for women of color. She also published *On Intersectionality: Essential Writings,* a book I highly recommend. I'm so grateful to Kimberlé for helping the world understand Intersectionality. I have often felt a personal struggle at the crossroads, but I didn't have the words to explain it to other people, especially to White people.

This is my own personal interpretation of the word. "Intersectionality" is when a person faces more than one threat of prejudice and/or discrimination based on specific aspects or characteristics of their identity. For example, an older Mexican woman who is poor, lesbian, and disabled may find herself being discriminated against for her age, race, gender, socioeconomic status, sexual preference, and disability. If she lives in a small rural town in the South, she may also face geographic location prejudice and discrimination, and possibly language discrimination if English is not her first language. This is Intersectionality at its finest, and at some point, we all find ourselves at the crossroads of being prejudged or mistreated based on who we are and how others perceive us. If you were this woman and you felt like you were being discriminated against in, for example, a department store, which part of your identity would be the victim, and what would you do about it? Which part of your identity would you fight for?

In other words, would the discrimination be due to you being female, Mexican, or disabled? It's hard to say, right? Well, no doubt this happens to many women every day worldwide, and I'm sure it has happened to you. But what does any of this have to do with you and whether you are an Antagonist, Advocate, or Ally? I want to address an issue very specific to you and me, and shed some light on an ongoing debate and challenge about feminism occurring within the feminist movement. Specifically, I'll be addressing feminism, the feminist movement, and women of color and Black women.

Let me refresh your memory about the feminist movement from its beginnings up until the current day. I also suggest you take a walk down memory lane by doing a bit of research for yourself. The intention for this chapter is not to provide you with a full lesson on the women's movement, but to share some highlights to further my discussion on Intersectionality and what it has to do with being an Antagonist, Advocate, or Ally.

Your research will reveal to you that the feminist movement started as far back as the fourteenth century in France, during the French Revolution. But feminism really began planting its roots in the Western part of the world in the late nineteenth century. It was spawned by middle- to upper-class White women who were seeking political equality and addressing the issue of "suffrage" (voting rights) for women.

The feminist movement in the United States, some Western European countries, and Canada sought to battle issues such as politics, reproductive rights, abortion, wage equity, socioeconomic disparities, and other inequalities between women and men. As you know, the women's movement was focused on challenging and breaking down barriers resulting from a dominant patriarchal society in the U.S. and abroad. We had some amazing and resilient women who fought hard on our behalf, and thanks to them, we now have many more rights and opportunities than we did. One thing is for sure, we are standing on the shoulders of some brave and fierce women.

I'd like to zero in on a particular moment in the women's movement that took place in the United States. Let's flash back to the years 1869 and 1870. Susan B. Anthony and Elizabeth Cady Stanton, who were big names in the women's suffrage movement, found themselves at an interesting intersection, the crossroads between gender and race. In 1870, Congress passed the 15th Amendment, which gave Black men—but no women of any color—the right to vote. Anthony and Stanton became resentful, and their deep bitterness began to endanger the women's movement. This was particularly true for the White women activists in the Southern states.

Susan B. Anthony was adamant about fighting for women's rights, so much so that she made this statement when the 15th Amendment was passed: *"I will cut off this right arm of mine before I will ever work or demand the ballot for the Negro and not the woman."* Of course, this statement, combined with the resentment of White women suffrage activists, created an intersection between gender and race. Although Black women and White women desired the same outcome (equality for women), many became divided at the crossroads that would forever change the dynamics of the women's movement. This planted the deep-seated resentment between Black women and White women that still exists today. According to Anthony and Stanton, it was all good while they were fighting for gender rights, but during the time of blatant racism and discrimination, **they were very much aligned with maintaining White Supremacy.** To be quite honest, Anthony and Stanton became belligerent in their refusal to allow or support the rights of Black men to vote, and the women's movement became poisoned with prejudice and racism.

Anthony was so aggressive in her pursuit of women's voting rights that she aligned with George Train, who was

pro-slavery. They began an ugly and hateful campaign to win women's voting rights with no regard to Black women's feelings and rights. Anthony is known for making countless racist remarks during this time, which further divided Black and White women. On one occasion, Anthony and Stanton wrote:

> *"We say not another man, Black or White, until woman is inside the citadel. What reason have we to suppose the African would be more just and generous than the Saxon has been?...how insulting to put every shade and type of manhood above our heads, to make laws for educated refined, wealthy women... The old anti-slavery school says women must stand back and wait until the Negroes shall be recognized. But we say, if you will not give the whole loaf of suffrage to the entire people, give it to the most intelligent first. If intelligence, justice, and morality are to have precedence in the government, let the question of the woman be brought up first and that of the Negro last...There is not the woman born who desires to eat the bread of dependence, no matter whether it be from the hand of father, husband, or brother; or any one who does so eat her bread places herself in the power of the person from whom she take it."*

> *—Susan B. Anthony and Elizabeth Cady Stanton*

Many women today are not aware of this moment when Susan B. Anthony and Elizabeth Cady Stanton were so determined to win that they lost on many levels. There's more I could share about the Anthony and Stanton story, but I'll leave that for your homework, as this is not meant to be a history lesson. What I will say is that history like this—history so deeply rooted in White Privilege, racism, and prejudice—is the cause of many of the world's problems today, especially in the modern women's movement. Surprisingly, at one time Susan B. Anthony was an anti-slavery activist, yet when someone is presented with the crossroads of Intersectionality, they are often forced to make a choice, whether it be race, gender, sexual preference, or religion. For Anthony and Stanton, the obvious choice was race. They couldn't fathom a Black man having rights they did not have, even in the strong patriarchal system and culture they lived in.

Black women, many still living under the rules of slavery, racism, and oppression, knew they had to create their own women's movement. It was obvious that two of the heavy hitters were **not willing** to fight for the rights of Black people. This division resulted in the formation of the National Association of Colored Women (NACW), led and championed by women such as Ida B. Wells, Sojourner Truth, and Mary Church Terrell. The National Woman Suffrage Association (NAWSA) was active at the same time, and was primarily comprised of **White women who did not want Black women attending their clubs and being part of their movement.**

During the 1913 Women's Suffrage Parade, Black women were asked to march in a different, segregated unit. Ida B. Wells was not having it! During the parade, she emerged from the crowd and took her *rightful place* at the front of the march, alongside the White women. Finally, in 1920, the 19th Amendment was passed, and it legally enfranchised *all* women, Black and White. **For at least a decade, many White women, including Anthony and Stanton, intentionally disenfranchised Black women through state laws and statutes and other exclusionary tactics.** In the end, Black women emerged victorious, but not without suffering through pain, struggle, and emotional oppression.

What does this have to do with you in the 21st century? More than you can imagine. And before you whip out your history books to debate what I've shared so far about the early days of the women's movement, save yourself some time and energy. Certainly, I don't know about *every* single woman, but I am very much aware of the many contributions made by various races of women who have fought for women's rights. You might even be thinking, *"What in the heck does any of this history have to do with me personally?"* **The division, whether it be silent and unspoken or loud and in your face, is still very much alive in today's New Age women's movement.** Sure, the movement has become more diverse and more inclusive, but there is still a division that many women either fear talking about, refuse to talk about, or don't know how to talk about. Well, I don't have any of those issues, so let's talk about it!

The crossroads that were faced in the early women's movement is still being encountered by women today, especially women of color and Black women. When you think about the modern women's empowerment movement, which leaders come to mind? I'm talking about those who are active and relevant today. Let me see if I can read your mind a bit. Maybe you are thinking of Brené Brown, Marianne Williamson, Hillary Clinton, or Sheryl Sandberg. Perhaps Oprah Winfrey, Michelle Obama, Taylor Swift, Iyanla Vanzant, or Ho Ching come to mind. The list is exhaustive and fairly diverse, globally speaking, for sure. Now let's look at another sector in the women's empowerment industry. I specifically want to examine the modern women's entrepreneurial empowerment industry. So, I'm talking about community leaders and entrepreneurs who are often speakers, coaches, and consultants, such as Danielle LaPorte, Marie Forleo, Gabby Bernstein, Ali Brown, Amy Porterfield, Mari

Smith, and Tory Johnson. I could continue to add to the list, but this is sufficient. Maybe you've heard of some of these women, and maybe you haven't.

What's my point with these women's empowerment leaders? Before I explain, the next time you are online, go to Google and type in the following phrases and view the images that pop up: "top female entrepreneurs," "top female life coaches," and "top female speakers." Take it a step farther and click on the first website listed for each category, and just browse around and see what you discover. Sure, you're going to see a sprinkling of women of color on some of those lists and in some of the images, but you'll mostly see White women. We've come a long way, but we still have a longer way to go.

There is still great disparity in the women's empowerment arena, and race and ethnicity are part of that disparity. Test it out for yourself. When you think of "top" female entrepreneurs, life coaches, experts, thought leaders, and speakers, do women of color come to mind, or do you really have to think about it? Continue to test the theory by paying attention to the social media marketing posts that begin with phrases like, "the industry's TOP whatever-type-of-expert." Click on the links, and notice that it's very clear who is included in the lineup and who is not. The question is, why? White women are still viewed as the "norm" and as the "experts," gurus, and thought leaders on all things female and feminist, and they often intentionally do not include women of color into their thoughts, visions, missions, programs, or events. Yet many will say they stand for, advocate for, and empower ALL women. **Pay attention to who is on the platforms for women, what they are speaking about, and who they are speaking for.**

I remember the moment when Marianne Williamson

announced she was running for Congress. The Internet exploded with excitement from women all over the United States and the world. Facebook and Twitter went crazy! For weeks and weeks, it seemed like her announcement was the only thing women were talking about. While I cannot say whether other women of color were excited, **I can share that I was not moved. I did not experience one ounce of delight.** Instead, the first thought that came to mind was, *"Will she speak for me, and will she speak for us?"* By "us," I meant women of color and Black women. No, I do not have exact numbers and didn't concern myself with gathering any, but it appeared to me—at least from my Facebook feed—that most of my women of color friends were not as excited about the announcement as many of my White friends were. I wondered if they were feeling and thinking the same thing I was: *"Will she speak for us?"* **My deeper question was, would she be an Antagonist, Advocate, or Ally?**

I'll admit I didn't put too much effort into delving deeper into the answer to that question; plus, I would have to engage with her personally to discover the true answer. I read various articles, listened to a few of her speeches, watched several of her campaign videos, and kept my eyes open for what was being said online and in the media. I decided to spend some time on her campaign website, and I noticed there was a page entitled "10 Reasons to Vote for Marianne." The reasons included getting money out of politics, women's rights, reclaiming democracy, quality education, the eradication of child poverty, eliminating mass incarceration, the dismantling of the National Security Agency (NSA), food corruption, advocating for peace and ending war, and lastly, her proclamation of being one of the most progressive Democrats running for Congress. A wonderful and noble list of intentions. I'm sure I would directly and indirectly benefit greatly from all her intentions; no doubt we all would. But there was nothing on her website, in her talks, or in her campaign marketing materials that screamed out, *"Yes, Catrice, I will be a voice for you, I will be an Ally to end the social and racial inequalities that plague women of color and Black women, on a daily basis."* Although fighting for women's rights was on her agenda, it was not convincing enough. **I didn't feel *included* in her agenda, because once again, there I stood at the crossroads, making the choice between gender and race.**

And now time has passed, and Marianne is running for President. Sadly, it has become clear that she remains oblivious to what it really means to be an Ally for women of color and Black women. She published an article on the *Huffington Post* titled "Race and Repentance in America." It was a great article, made excellent points, and overall it was a wonderful message. She definitely "talks the talk," but I would love to see her doing more walking than talking. In other words, she could show up and be active when Black men are being gunned down in the streets by White officers, when Black churches are being burned, and the other moments when women of color and Black women need her the most. I do appreciate the work Marianne is doing in the world; she is definitely an Advocate. Marianne, if you're listening, please show up more for women of color and Black women!

Just like the old school women's movement, the modern-day women's movement—by and large, knowingly and unknowingly—still creates a crossroads for women of color and Black women. If the modern women's movement does not awaken to this truth and actively operate as an Ally, the crossroads will always be there. Women of color and Black women will have to make the *unnecessary* choice between gender and race. I've heard many White women wonder why Black people, Black women, have created their own communities and networks, such as BET (Black Entertainment Television), Black Girls Rock!, the National Council of Negro Women, and so many others.

The reason is very simple: since the days of Susan B. Anthony and Elizabeth Cady Stanton, it's been clear that **although we may be invited, we are not necessarily included.** You'll notice this to be true of other races and ethnicities as well. Latina, Asian, Native, and Indigenous women have had to start their own missions, movements, communities, and networks because they too were invited but not included. Have you ever noticed that there are not (at least I don't know about them) any White women's organization? For example, you don't hear about the National Council of White Women, nor is there WET (White Entertainment Television). **That's because *everything else* that is not specifically designated for us is designated for you.** It is assumed, presumed, and the truth that if people of color really felt invited, wanted, accepted, seen, honored, respected, and appreciated, they would have never had to create these communities and networks.

Let me tell you about a modern day *Wonder Woman*. A woman who not only found herself at the crossroads of Intersectionality, but gained world-wide instant fame because she chose to blaze down *Race Lane* with her superhero cape on! Like many women of color and Black women, she was **sick and tired of being sick and tired**, yet refused to give up the good fight against social and racial injustice and racism. Brittany "Bree" Newsome is a bodacious and brave Black woman who audaciously climbed up the flag pole in Charleston, South Carolina on June 28, 2015 at the break of dawn to personally remove the Confederate flag from the South Carolina State House. Bree Newsome instantly became a social media rock star. She was eventually arrested and charged for defacing a monument.

Bree was a #BlackLivesMatter activist, and after the shooting at Emanuel African Methodist Episcopal Church in Charleston, where nine innocent Black church members were gunned down and killed by Dylan Roof, a racist terrorist, Bree had had enough! Shortly after being released from jail, she said, *"I did it for all the fierce Black women on the front lines of the movement and for all the little Black girls who are watching us. I did it because I am free."* I was so moved by her courage and fearless leadership that I knew I too must step up to be braver about racial justice issues. I knew Bree had to be included in this book. How does Bree's story fit into this chapter? Bree is like many other Black women who daily find themselves at the crossroads, the intersection between gender and race.

I cannot read Bree's mind (oh, how I'd love to), but I'm pretty sure while standing at the intersection of her womanhood and Blackness, she felt compelled to choose the more important road. Imagine her standing at a fork in the road called *My Reality Road,* where she could go right onto *Feminist Avenue,* left onto *Race Lane,* straight ahead onto *Minding My Own Business Parkway,* or turn around and go back on *Same Ol' Shit Street.* This fork in the road called Intersectionality is a daily soul stop for many women of color and Black women. **Life is constantly bringing us to this place in our daily journey through life, even when we have no intention or desire to be there.** We simply want to travel the path of Mind My Own Business Parkway as we pursue our purposes and live out our daily lives. Yet the oppressive and painful pull of social and racial injustices against women of color and Black women tug at our minds, bodies, and spirits, and beckon us to begrudgingly return to that same crossroads. Bree passionately and purposely chose to take a left turn onto *Race Lane.* Why? According to statements she has made, she felt like she *had* to travel that path and face racism head on by removing the Confederate flag, which for many Black people is a symbol of slavery, hate, and racism.

Sure, Bree could have easily kept straight on *Minding My Own Business Parkway*. In other words, she could have just ignored the disrespectful act of South Carolina keeping the Confederate flag up and not lowering it to half-staff as a result of nine of their Black citizens being victims of a hate crime. She could have gone back on *Same Ol' Shit Street*, but she chose to courageously defend her race. This is important for you to understand, because we women of color, Black women must make these kinds of choices every single day of our lives, and often several times in one day. **And nine times out of ten, we will choose to defend our race, because it is always under attack.** We're often plagued with the pain of protecting and preserving our race, standing up and speaking out about our race, and guarding our livelihood from the racial prejudice, discrimination, and racism we encounter because of something we cannot fix or change: our skin color. And many of us love the skin we are in!

As Bree's story shows, we often must choose race over gender, a luxury that White women often take for granted or deny they even have the privilege of doing. On very rare occasions, White women may have to choose *Race Lane*, but not very often. Why? **Because the White race is not under daily attack.** How often are you at the crossroads? When is the last time you had to make the decision to choose your race over your gender? We are tired of having to make this choice!

We, like you, just want to travel down *Minding My Own Business Parkway* and live our lives, but that is not possible when we are serving a life sentence of "living while Black or brown." **We're also tired of biting our tongue, tucking our tail,** numbing our feelings, holding our breath, and suffering in silence. We're exhausted by trying to explain it to White people, and we're fed up with being angry, which is what happens when we choose to turn around and go back down *Same Ol' Shit Street.* Going back down this path means we ignore racist remarks, dismiss discrimination, lash out when we've had enough, avoid deep race talks with White people, become desensitized to the daily racial attacks our people experience, and the list could go on and on. It's tiring just thinking about everything else I could type here.

What does this have to do with you? *In my lifetime, I've been at the crossroads more with White women than White men by a landslide.* This has been the intersection of my life, my whole life. Remember Marty in Chapter One? Ever since the day he asked why my skin was dirty, the intersection between gender and race has been my reality. It will be my reality until I take my last breath, unless of course White people dismantle racism and close Pandora's box, their cruel creation. **If you say you are a feminist or a women's empowerment champion, but refuse to admit and own your White Privilege, then YOU are a liar and an oppressor of women, especially women of color and Black women.** Please stop hiding behind the facade of feminism, step forward into the light, tell the truth, set yourself free, and use your power to pull the plug on racism. Stop tossing the word "feminism" around if you have no knowledge of what happens at the crossroads of Intersectionality. While you're at it, I hope you take the advice Flavia Dzodan shares in her infamous article: *"My feminism will be intersectional or it will be bullshit."*

Racism is a social problem that White people must take the lead in solving, and it all begins with admitting

to, owning, and using your White Privilege to break down racism one invisible and visible brick at a time. Will you sit back as an Antagonist and watch this system grow stronger and stronger? Will you sit on the fence as an Advocate, picking and choosing when you act or show up? Or will you first tear down your own White Picket Fence, pick up a sledgehammer, and start from the basement up to demolish racism? The choice is always yours! Oh, and by the way, while you're deciding: Black and brown people are dying all over the world... because of White Privilege and racism.

WAKE-UP CALL QUESTIONS

What makes it so difficult, uncomfortable, or terrifying for you to talk candidly about race and racism?

_____

_____

_____

_____

_____

_____

Why do you struggle to own ALL your White Privilege, and what do you think will happen when you do?

_____

_____

_____

_____

_____

_____

_____

_____

How have you failed to truly SEE women of color and Black women for who they really are, and FAILED THEM, behind the guise of "I don't see color"?

_____

_____

_____

_____

_____

_____

How are you living the lie? Do you say you empower ALL women? Do you say your programs and services are inclusive when they're not? How are you going to start living in truth by understanding and avoiding collisions at the crossroads between race and gender?

_____

_____

_____

_____

_____

_____

_____

_____

Chapter 7

THE MISAPPROPRIATION OF CULTURE

"What would America be like if we loved Black people as much as we love Black culture?"

—*Amandla Stenberg*

If you went into a store and took a dress just to wear it for a special occasion, and then you returned it, is that stealing? You didn't mean any harm; you were just borrowing it and giving it back once you didn't need it anymore. You were taking it only for a specific purpose, so you weren't really stealing. You felt like it was okay because the dress was cheap, and you could get the same style just about everywhere. It wasn't like you were borrowing an expensive dress. The store must not really need it; they have so many in stock. You even kept the tag intact so it could be sold. You don't think the dress will lose any value, because you're going to give it back. You see it as a win-win: you get to borrow the dress and return it, and the store gets to sell it. Agree or disagree? Is this right?

THIS is wrong on so many levels, and most people would

agree with me. Any time you take something without asking or being given permission, it's stealing. Period! **Just because you didn't *intend* any harm, doesn't mean you didn't *cause* any harm.** Just because you are compelled to satisfy or fulfill a personal purpose doesn't give you the right to take or borrow something that doesn't belong to you. The cost of what you borrow or steal may seem insignificant, but it was still of value to the original owner. Just because you see the dress all over the place and it's easily accessible doesn't give you the right to take it. Taking something, "using" it, and then giving it back always decreases the value of what you've stolen. Would you agree?

Whenever you take or borrow something that doesn't belong to you, *it is stealing*, and thus there is both a perpetrator and a *victim*. This is just as true for a dress in a department store as it is for one race borrowing, taking, or stealing someone else's culture. It is *highly* disrespectful and offensive for anyone who is not Native American or does not belong to an Indigenous tribe to wear a headpiece or any other culturally specific item or garment. Dressing up like a geisha, a Jewish rabbi, or an Arab prime minister on Halloween is distasteful, insensitive, and offensive. I could go on and on and give examples of why **"borrowing" someone else's cultural heritage is a disrespectful no-no,** but let's shift gears for a minute. I will return to this point later in this chapter.

Exploring and experiencing different cultures is a beautiful thing. Participating in cultural events such as watching a Cinco de Mayo parade, celebrating Black History Month, attending a pow wow, and celebrating Chinese New Year can be very rewarding as a participant, but there's a fine line you do not want to cross. There is a big difference between appreciating a culture and embezzling a culture. When you *appreciate* something or someone, you see the value; you adore the divine essence and respect the person or thing for what it truly is. When you *embezzle*, you take something for granted, steal it, and you often discard it when it's no longer of use to you.

Let's talk about two of the biggest and most notorious White female thieves of culture and offenders of cultural racism in the music industry today: Katy Perry and Miley Cyrus. Economic exploitation is the name of the game for these two. They borrow and steal African American culture to increase their visibility, fame, and economic status; they exploit women of color and Black women; and then, when it's no longer convenient or they've gained what they desired, they take off the costume, drop the dialect, and go back to being White, where they *still* own and have access to all their *unearned* privileges. That isn't even the worst part. **Every time a culture is robbed and embezzled, that culture and ethnic heritage become diluted and deemed theft-worthy for any other self- serving thief to come along and take what they want, when they want, and as often as they want.**

African women have been "twerking" or doing what are called *"African isolation"* moves for centuries. Historically, Black women have been known to be rhythmic in their bodies, which can be traced back to their ancestral roots. Since being sold into slavery and arriving in America, Black women's bodies have not been their own. The Black woman's body has been ridiculed, shamed, raped, beaten, and mocked for centuries. Let me introduce you to Sarah Baartman. Sarah Baartman, born in 1789, was an African slave who was most famous for being known as the "Hottentot Venus" in the nineteenth century. The offensive word "Hottentot" was first applied to African/Black people in the late seventeenth century by White Europeans in reference to the members of the Khoikhoi Indigenous tribe in South Africa. Sarah Baartman was given the name "Hottentot Venus," a **highly derogatory** phrase, because White Europeans considered her physical features grotesque.

Sarah was exhibited at "freak shows" for her extremely large buttocks, disproportionately sized genitalia, and exotic skin. She was then sold to an English doctor and spent four years in Britain being put on display for the world to gawk at and make fun of her butt. After being sold to a Frenchman, the inhumane exhibitions continued in Paris, where onlookers were freely able to mock and laugh at her body even after her death. Her body was dissected and put on display for people to view her brain, skeleton, and genitalia until she was finally buried. Sarah's body was considered abnormal and exotic—she was said to have looked like an orangutan—thus, society considered her to be a *wild and savage* female. Sarah *"Hottentot"* Baartman was considered to be more ape-like than human; she and her curvaceous body were deemed inhuman and animalistic. She was an object of ridicule and "scientific" inquiry until she took her last breath in 1816. Sadly, her skeleton and body cast remained on display in France until 1976. For nearly two hundred years, from 1789 until 1976, her body was not only despicably displayed, but was also used to promote the world view of the Black woman's body as lifeless, unlovable, lewd, and free to be lasciviously looted.

The animalistic perceptions of the Black woman's body did not end with the death of Sarah Baartman; it continues today. When Serena Williams won the 2015 Wimbledon championship, her muscular physique immediately became part of the discussion when many haters claimed it was her "manly" muscles that allowed her to dominate among female tennis players. For decades, she has been scrutinized and taunted with hateful words like "gorilla," "manly," and "savage," including by her White female peers. In 2012, her White peer Caroline Wozniacki stuffed her sports bra and shorts to imitate Serena during a match against Maria Sharapova, while the crowd laughed and thought it was hilarious. Sounds a bit like the taunting Sarah Baartman endured, doesn't it? **And let me make this point: the taunting and dehumanizing behavior is inflicted by women just as much as it is by men,** and her *Blackness* is more disturbing and despised by the hecklers and haters than her *manly-ness* is.

Serena Williams and other Black women often experience what I call "triple trauma": a deadly combination of personal attacks rooted in misogyny, racism, and transphobia. **The Black woman's body (and spirit) is always under attack.** Our bodies have been sexualized, dehumanized, and exoticized, and with every breath we take, we grapple with our womanhood at the intersection of sexism and racism. You see, no matter how much fame and money Serena obtains, she CANNOT escape the Black skin she is in.

So it's highly irrelevant and offensive to me when I hear White women say, *"I know how you feel; I was born poor, grew up poor, and had to work hard for everything I have, so there's no way I can be privileged."* **Just having White skin is a prestigious and profitable privilege. Period!** While I was contemplating the cover design for this book, I asked a "White" (White-skinned, White-appearing) friend of mine to give me some feedback on the two cover options. She gave her feedback and suggested the one she preferred. I asked if the cover and title alone were enough to intrigue her to pick up the book and read it, and she said yes. She then mentioned she was of "mixed race," and thus her feedback may not be very relevant because the book was written for "White" women. Curious, I asked her, *"So how do you identify yourself?"* She said she was a mixture of Filipino, Native American, Italian, and Spanish, and that she usually checks "Other" on the racial identity box. Honestly, I didn't know that about her; she looks White.

I thought, *"Boy, it must be nice to BE those ethnicities, yet show up looking White, and to have the luxury of checking 'Other,' but still get all the social privileges of being White in society's eyes."* I can check "Other" all I want, but I don't have the luxury and privilege to show up and move around in the world as an "Other." No matter what I believe I am, and regardless of what box I check, to society and the world I AM a Black woman. **This, my friend, is a perfect example of White Privilege.** And while I love this woman dearly, I don't think she realizes the power of her privilege, nor does she understand what she really said to me. Truth is, this book is relevant to her. I hope she reads it and chooses to become a full-fledged Ally!

Sure, White Privilege is anchored in one's ethnicity and genealogical roots, but physical identity and social perception play a part as well. The power of White Privilege is in the profitable "passing." Looking, appearing, showing up as, and being perceived as White is where the privilege lies. White Privilege is the byproduct of race. And remember, "race" is a social construct created to categorize a set of similar characteristics to identify a group of people. The White race was created by White people to seize and maintain social, political, religious, and economic power. I suggest you read up on the creation of Whiteness to learn more. Chapter Eight includes an excerpt from an article by Audrey Smedley that discusses the creation of "race," and the Resources for the Journey section includes books that discuss the creation of the "White race." Rachel Dolezal, the White woman who "passed" as a Black woman and eventually became the president of the National Association for the Advancement of Colored People (NAACP) in Spokane, Washington, "believed" she was a Black woman. She "looked" like a light-skinned Black woman, a mixed-race woman who appeared to be Black. Therefore, the perception was that she was indeed Black. Although her biological roots and DNA may prove otherwise, once Rachel chose to "pass" in the world, the world saw her as a Black woman regardless of her genealogy. It really doesn't matter what Rachel's true motive for passing was; her passing was much more than a personal fantasy of cultural fulfillment. **Her passing was racial identity theft.** And because of the Jim Crow Era's *one-drop rule*, which stated that if a White person had a single drop of Black blood in their genealogy, they were considered to be Black and a second-class citizen, Rachel was allowed to "pass."

Rachel Dolezal, a cultural thief, "stole" an identity that was not hers for the taking. Her manufactured Blackness is the perfect example of the derogatory act of "Blackface" and definitely a slap in the face of Black people and especially Black women. She stole and raped Black identity and culture, but whenever she chooses to, she can return to *Privilegeville* and reap the rewards and benefits of being White. Why did Rachel Dolezal pose as a Black woman? The answer is quite simple: **she believed it was her God-given right to do so.** Thievery, plagiarism, exploitation, imitation, bastardization, raping, pillaging, and/or cultural genocide come from a deep systemic belief of superiority and White Entitlement. **Rachel and all the other cultural imposters in the world believe they have the right to steal and rape the cultures of people of color; that's what America was built upon.**

Ever since what is known as North America was infiltrated by White explorers, conquerors, and settlers, people of color have been brutally informed that White is right, and if your skin is not White, you don't matter, you have little to no value, and anything that belongs to you will be forcibly taken, even your life. I'll leave the rest of that history lesson for you to explore.

Now, do not confuse what Rachel, Miley, and Katy are doing with what are known as *assimilation* and *acculturation*. "Assimilation" is more than likely what your ancestors did when they arrived in America. Many European immigrants came to the United States for a shot at a better life and to flee the socioeconomic constraints of their native land. Millions of Irish people flooded America in the nineteenth century, and during their quest for a "good life," they learned how to fit in, blend in, and adapt so they could assimilate into American society. Many lost their lives due to discrimination, and far more lost their identity as they chose to divorce themselves from much of their culture to be "accepted" into White America.

Today, Irish Americans are said to "sit at the top of the socioeconomic table and are one of the most prosperous ethnic groups in America." *Assimilation mission is complete!* What do I mean? Assimilation happens when ethnic or marginalized people become "absorbed into" the dominant culture and systems. The Irish, once viewed as despicable outcasts, have not only blended in, but have become a large proportion of the American White race. The benefit of having White skin has allowed the Irish, Italian, Swedish, Scottish, English, and other White or light-skinned people to effectively assimilate into the dominant (aka White) cultural and social systems, and only because they are considered to be White.

It was a big deal when John F. Kennedy, a man of Irish descent, ran for President. But no one seems to notice or care that Joe Biden is Irish Catholic. Nancy Pelosi, the first Italian American to be the Speaker of the House, got little to no backlash about being Italian, but faced a lot of criticism for being a woman. This is assimilation at its finest. This is the epitome of White Privilege. So sure, many other "White" ethnic groups have experienced prejudice, discrimination, and social and human injustices, but eventually they acculturated and became part of the dominant White culture.

They quickly realized that forfeiting their ethnicity granted them the ultimate golden ticket, the induction into the White race. This is certainly not the case for our Black and brown sisters and brothers. No matter how hard they try to assimilate into White America, White America can SEE their ethnicity from head to toe. There is no escaping the skin they live and breathe in. So, while I have empathy for the pain, hate, and discrimination that White ethnic groups have experienced, life is dramatically different and overwhelmingly oppressive for women of color and Black women, who can't, even if they want to, deny or forfeit their ethnicity.

Acculturation happens when ethnic or marginalized groups or individuals become well-versed and highly adaptive to the dominant culture and social systems. Notice the difference. "Assimilation" means you've been absorbed into the dominant culture, while "acculturation" means you've learned how to survive within the dominant culture. Now isn't that interesting? **Those who have the right skin color can assimilate, blend in, and ultimately thrive if they choose to, while those who do not have the right skin color can at best survive.** And even when they choose to thrive, they NEVER escape racism. **Race trumps everything!** Barack Obama is a Black man who was President and Commander in Chief of the United States, and still he will never escape the skin he is in. He will survive, just like the rest of us people of color do, but he won't thrive. Why not? Because thriving is far more complex than sitting in the Oval Office, driving a million-dollar car, sleeping in a mansion, and/or having a six- or seven-figure income. You can have all those things, but if you are not socially free from hate, racism, discrimination, and oppression, you are NOT truly thriving on an emotional, psychological, or spiritual level. **White Privilege will not allow Barack Obama or any other person of color to be truly free and thrive**

like we DESERVE to.

So again, what does it mean to be White? What are the cultures and traditions of White people? Many White people can't answer those questions because they have given up their ethnicity in exchange for the golden ticket. And many golden-ticket holders eventually discover that although their ticket opens many socioeconomic doors, it also closes and locks the doors that hold their true identity, the soul of who they really are. Unconsciously and consciously, these people seek to identify with something culturally real, something that will connect them to their truth. They soon realize their culture may be lost forever; their ethnicity has been sacrificed for White Supremacy and entrance into the White race club. So, what does the golden-ticket holder do? They rob, steal, and rape other people's ethnicity and culture simply because, as a golden-ticket holder (aka a White person), they can. History has taught us that White people, by virtue of their White skin, have been granted the privilege and power to continue to rape the cultures of people of color, and the people themselves. So, let's get back to Katy Perry and Miley Cyrus. Love them or hate them, they are capitalizing on and cashing in on the embezzlement of Black culture (and others) by raping and pillaging the language, dialect, dance moves, hair styles, and whatever else they feel entitled to take.

Since arriving in this country forcibly or by choice, the Black woman has been raped from head to toe repeatedly. Her native tongue and language have been silenced, her body assaulted and dehumanized, her breast milk siphoned for profit (a literal cash cow), her name taken as if she never existed. If that isn't enough, she's also been criticized for her curves, mocked for the melanin in her skin, taunted for the tight curls in her hair, laughed

at for her luscious lips and wave-like hips, villainized for her voice, and given the side-eye of discrimination for her cultural attire, hairstyles, and ethnic presence. Yet every Katy, Miley, and Rachel believe they can show up, flash their golden ticket, and capitalize on our culture to cash in emotionally, psychologically, physically, and economically. They enter once again into communities of color to rape, pillage, and embezzle the Black culture that we've had to fight and die to keep. The very same culture that when expressed in and on our Black bodies is deemed ugly, ghetto, hypersexual, animalistic, inhuman, and unpalatable. **Once White women have sucked the life out of our cultural belongings, they give them back, watered down and devalued, and then they flash their golden ticket and exit the Black community as if they never molested a race.** That's what the Misappropriation of Culture looks, feels, and sounds like!

Before you think you are nothing like Miley, Katy, or Rachel, let me share with you how the Misappropriation of Culture may show up in your life. At the root of cultural appropriation are deep-seated beliefs, illustrated by this partial list of justifications:

- *"Everyone else is doing it."*
- *"I'm not really stealing anything, I'm just borrowing it."*
- *"I can have everything else, so why not this too?"*
- *"They don't need it."*
- *"They won't care."*
- *"It's not really valuable."*
- *"It didn't cost them anything."*
- *"We've taken from them without permission or punishment before, so why not?"*

- *"It's a cool new trend."*
- *"The celebrities are doing it."*
- *"It's a great marketing strategy."*

Are you using your privilege to pillage? You are if you're a White woman who:

- *Is rocking cornrows and you think they are stylish and cute.*
- *Uses the term "sistah" as a term of endearment for your fellow White sisters (and if you're saying it to Black women, it's offensive).*
- *Uses the term "hood" (as in "my neighborhood") or the term "homegirl" (when referring to a friend).*
- *Uses the term "pow wow" to refer to a powerful meeting with your colleagues (a pow wow is a sacred Indigenous ceremony that is not to be mocked or White-washed).*
- *Dresses up in another culture's native and cultural attire for the sake of art, promotion, and/or casual daily dress (such as Native American headpieces, sarongs, and so on).*
- *Uses ethnic language or cultural slang in your branding and marketing materials.*

This is a short but important list of ways you may be using your privilege and power to pillage other people's cultures. The *taking* trivializes historical and current oppression. The *borrowing* allows you to try it on for fun but not have to deal with the fear, discrimination, and/or anxiety experienced by the oppressed people. The *casual use of it* affords you the opportunity to cash in on it, yet the culture it belongs to may be struggling financially.

When you take a piece of someone's culture and say to White people that *"it rocks," "it's epic,"* or *"oh, how edgy and fun it is,"* you deny the pain inflicted by the dominant group who says it's **"too Black, too urban, or too ethnic"** when people of color embody their own culture.

When you steal people's culture or just borrow it temporarily, you romanticize the struggles of that culture. And while you're just trying on, playing with, leveraging, capitalizing on, and/or having fun with other people's cultures, they are still being targeted, profiled, discriminated against, attacked, and oppressed. The bottom line is that if the item (whether it be dress, attire, language, or hairstyle) is NOT part of your own culture, check yourself and make sure you are expressing appreciation and not appropriation, and then double-check yourself, because it is a fine line.

- *How would you feel if someone stole your family heirlooms?*
- *How would you feel if people said to you, "I want to borrow your culture, but I hate you?"*
- *How would you feel if the stealing of your culture gave thieves all the rewards but no burdens?*
- *How would you feel if the taking of your culture allowed someone to profit while your people still live in poverty?*
- *How would you feel if the embezzlement of your culture minimized your pain, struggle, suffering, and ongoing oppression?*

You might be tempted to ask, *"Well, Catrice, what about people of color 'stealing' White culture?"* Let me answer you by asking this question of you again: *"What is White culture?"* And finally, this is the most pivotal point of the whole discussion. **When people**

in power, the dominant group (White people), adopt, use, or "borrow" the culture of people who have been systematically oppressed by the dominant group, there is a power dynamic involved that makes a significant difference. White people have not endured centuries of systemic racism and oppression, have not endured physical and cultural rape as a people at the hands of Black/brown people, and have not had to fight and die to preserve their culture and be treated as equals in America.

Therefore, the borrowing or adaptation of the dominant culture, White Supremacy, by people of color was (and is) critically necessary to live and survive. As long as White people hold the social and economic power in America, people of color will have to make the choice to acculturate, and often times it's a forced choice, especially if they want to get a good-paying job, rise out of poverty, and/or climb the socioeconomic ladder of success. There is so much more to say about this, but I'll leave it up to you to explore how White Privilege affects people of color on a daunting continuum.

Please *stop playing* with people's cultures unless you are willing to pay the price to defend those same cultures and racial ethnic groups with your blood, sweat, and tears. And to do anything other than pay that price is to dehumanize, bastardize, and rape cultures that have already been raped enough. Think about it like this. One single rape is horrifically bad enough. Just imagine how it feels to be gang-raped over and over and over and over... until you take your last breath. **The misuse of your power and the Misappropriation of Culture is a deadly concoction that slowly kills the human spirit. Don't be a perpetrator; instead, refuse to continue to perpetuate racism and oppression.** Failure to responsibly use the power of your privilege is lethal. You may not be physically killing people, but the reckless use of White Privilege undeniably kills people, one spirit at a time, even when the homicide is done unintentionally. This takes me back to this chapter's opening quote by Amandla Stenberg, who said, *"What would America be like if we loved Black people as much as we love Black culture?"* My response is, *"What would America be like if White people loved their own culture as much as they love the cultures of people of color?"*

WAKE-UP CALL QUESTIONS

Now that you know what Misappropriation of Culture is, how many times have you stolen, raped, or devalued the cultures of people of color?

_____

_____

_____

_____

_____

_____

What are you going to do to rediscover your own ethnicity and celebrate it?

_____

_____

_____

_____

_____

_____

_____

How will you begin to use your privilege to empower instead
of to pillage?

_____

_____

_____

_____

_____

_____

_____

How different would YOUR life be if you loved Black people as
much you love Black culture?

_____

_____

_____

_____

_____

_____

_____

"The only thing worse than a bigot is an 'Ally' who can't stop congratulating themselves on their enlightenment."

JULIO ALEXI GENAO

Chapter 8

BECOMING A WHITE ALLY

"If you are neutral in situations of injustice, you have chosen the side of the oppressor."

—Desmond Tutu

You may not want to believe it, but we are still in a civil war! The original American Civil War may have ended and been documented in the history books, but it's far from over. In many ways, it has started up again. You and I are part of this racial justice war, whether we know it or like it. Ironically, the war I speak of is very similar to the American Civil War that occurred from 1861 to 1865, when the United States was at war with itself. **Americans killing Americans.** Many White people do not want to believe or admit it, but the American Civil War was solely about slavery. Period. I suggest you do your own research, but let me summarize why I believe this truth.

Seven Southern slave states (states who believed in and upheld their right to own slaves, primarily African/Black people, human beings) declared their secession from the United States. They created what is known as the Confederate States of America (thus the Confederate flag), and were eventually joined by four other states. **This war's origin is clearly and undeniably about slavery.** The great debate was simple. Most Northerners (aka the Union) essentially did not want the horrific, inhumane business of slavery to continue and/or to expand into the Western states.

Southerners (aka the Confederacy) did want slavery to continue and expand, and **they felt they had every God-given right as states to buy, beat, rape, exploit, lynch, hang, kill, sodomize, terrorize, and sell people.** Black people. *Human beings.* The Confederacy believed the Union was infringing on their constitutional rights to buy, own, and sell slaves for financial gain. Before the war started, the Northern states were working to abolish slavery in the North and were hoping to continue their efforts throughout the U.S. The Southerners grew angrier and the Union refused to budge, and therefore, due to irreconcilable differences, Americans went to war against each other to fight both for and against slavery, America's *"national evil."*

You can add all the other reasons you believe the American Civil War ensued, but what you cannot deny is that the Southerners clearly and emphatically felt threatened by the Government, which was meddling in the Southerners' business of owning PEOPLE. Let that sink in. People, not land or livestock, but *people, human beings like you and your children.* The Confederate States of America was enraged that the Union was interfering with their "right" to take their slaves anywhere in the country and keep them in the *bondage of slavery*, even if they took them to a free, anti-slavery state. The Confederacy was livid that the Government was **compromising their cash flow by stating that owning PEOPLE, working them like damn dogs, beating and raping them, buying and selling them for pennies, impregnating them and** denying their children, sodomizing them, humiliating them, starving them and/or feeding them scraps and crap, killing their spirits, lynching their bodies, and whipping them bloody was wrong. The Confederacy disagreed, proclaiming that ALL this, and every other vile, sadistic, and devilish thing in between was their *God-given right,* and they could do whatever they wanted with their PROPERTY, including *raping and killing little Black girls and boys.*

You can dress it up with words like American history, heritage, national pride, brotherhood, state's rights, liberty, and citizen's rights all you want, but oh yes! The American Civil War was and *always will be about slavery,* believe it or deny it; the choice is yours. Just know the denial of it will reveal you to be an Antagonist, sitting behind your White Picket Fence. Let's take a step back for a minute to the last sentence in the paragraph above. Why would *anyone in their right mind* believe in, be in support of, and proudly wave a Confederate flag that represents not only **the raping and killing of little Black girls and boys,** but also EVERYTHING horrific that happened to Black people while enslaved by White people! **The thought of it is sickening, twisted, pathetic, pitiful, and sad.** Imagine those things happening *for centuries* to your sisters, brothers, husbands, uncles, aunts, grandparents, children, nieces, nephews, and grandchildren. And then imagine how you might feel when the Confederate flag is so arrogantly and recklessly waved in your face! (Dig deeper into this; hopefully you'll discover more truths.)

Oh yes, we are at war! The same war fought in the 1800s is still being fought today. It just sounds and looks different. But before I shed some light on that, let's go back to something else of significance. I stated in the Introduction that I wrote this guide specifically for White women because, first of all, I have been discriminated against and racially oppressed by more White women than White men. Second, I haven't focused on all women of color and ethnicities only because there's too much to cover in one book. But don't worry; it's part of my belief system and ongoing mission to speak for all women, especially women of color. Third, this book focuses on the social and racial relationships between White and Black women because that is the frame of reference I know best, and the one that, in my opinion, carries a significant amount of unaddressed, lingering, and unresolved pain and conflict. Let me expand my perspective.

African/Black slave women were not only forced to work in the fields, but they also served as **semen depositories for those good ol' Christian, upstanding pillars of the community, those wholesome fathers and adoring husbands, White men, who belonged to White women.** African/Black slave women were not only shamefully beaten in public when they failed to work like machines, they were also molested, savagely raped, impregnated, and sexually used and abused repeatedly. Many of the slavemasters' White wives knew all about their husbands' acts of sexual brutality and said NOTHING. They dared not shame themselves and their husbands in public.

African/Black slave women were not only responsible for taking care of their own children (the ones they had with their husbands or partners *and* the ones created and denied by the slavemaster), they were also responsible for taking care of the White woman: doing her cooking, cleaning her home, and caring for her White children. The White woman did *whatever the hell she wanted to* while the slave woman was taking care of the White woman's house and her man. **The African/Black slave woman was the White man's concubine and oftentimes the White woman's footstool and milk-producing maid.** It was mighty fine for an African/Black woman to breastfeed those White babies and care for them, but there was no reciprocity for the slave; her half-White and half-Black ("mulatto") children couldn't even step foot in the big house and were often mistreated. After all, the White woman knew that her man was those children's father.

Imagine an African/Black slave woman working in the hot fields all day alongside the men, then waiting on the White woman hand and foot, being the victim of her *rape of the day* by the White man, and finally—maybe—getting a free moment to herself and her family. Tired, emotionally beat down, spiritually hopeless waiting on God to show up and save her, she also had to breastfeed the White woman's babies. The unapproved and unwanted taking of her mind, body, and soul occurred repeatedly. But don't take my word for this; come out from behind the White Picket Fence and make your way to the library for an additional history lesson that should enlighten you, wake you up, and help you become more socially conscious. The following passage from *Once a Slave: The Slave's View of Slavery,* a book by Stanley Feldstein, supports what I believe to be true, and depicts just a snapshot of the master-slave relationship and the consequences of simply living in Black skin:

> *"Maria was a thirteen-year-old house servant. One day, receiving no response to her call, the mistress began searching the house for her. Finally, she opened the parlor door, and there was the child with her master. The master ran out of the room, mounted his horse and rode off to escape, 'though well he knew that [his wife's] full fury would fall upon the young head of his victim.' The mistress beat the child and locked her up in a smokehouse. For two weeks the girl was constantly whipped. Some of the elderly servants attempted to plead with the mistress on Maria's behalf, and even hinted*

that 'it was mass'r that was to blame.' The mistress's reply
was typical: 'She'll know better in the future. After I've done
with her, she'll never do the like again, through "ignorance."'

—Stanley Feldstein, Once a Slave: The Slave's View of Slavery

This pedophilic assault on young girls by the White man, the slavemaster, happened too many times to count or document. Let us not forget that young **Black boys were assaulted and raped by White female pedophiles too,** and that while the White man of the house was away, many Black men and boys were forced to have sex with the White woman, the wife, the mistress. **Rape after rape, assault after assault; yes, this all happened, and oftentimes the White woman said nothing or did very little about it.** After all, White women back then couldn't always take care of themselves and needed the financial support of their men, their husbands. And after all, divorce was not a common practice, so White women stayed in marriages they would have preferred to escape. **And after all, these superficial, self-serving reasons the White women had for staying quiet and married were what legitimized and justified not only keeping silent, but also participating in the horrific dehumanization of African/Black people.**

African/Black slave men dared not defend their wives, sisters, daughters, or mothers unless they wanted to face death. Many did anyway, and rightfully so. What's ironic is those same African/Black slave men also dared not even look at, speak to, or walk on the same side of the road as a White woman, unless they wanted to be whipped to death or lynched. *Well, isn't that hypocritical!* White men and women could do whatever they wanted, whenever they wanted, and as savagely as they wanted to African/Black men and women, but when the roles were reversed, then humiliation, beatings, and death were the consequence. But mind you, these weren't just regular ol' White folks, they were Bible-teaching and preaching Christians, upstanding citizens, and great pillars of the community—and also statutory rapists. I appreciate the naked truth of the following passages from Failing Our Black Children: Statutory Rape Laws, Moral Reform and the Hypocrisy of Denial, a book by Gloria J. Browne-Marshall:

"Powerless against a lustful husband and blind to the harsh realities of chattel slavery, the enraged wife often vented her jealous rage upon the one person whom she could control, the black woman."

"Colonial laws regarding statutory rape were not applied to Blacks and Indians. Indians and Blacks, as well as their children, were prohibited by law from defending themselves against abuse, sexual and otherwise, at the hands of Whites. A slave who defended herself against the attack of a White person was subject to cruel beatings by either the master or mistress. Liaisons between Whites and Blacks or Indians were illegal. The females of color received the harshest punishment if discovered in a liaison with a White male. Females of color, regardless of their young age, were viewed as seducers of White men. Pregnancy became the evidence of the illegal liaison. A mulatto baby the indicator of the race of the father— White male. The child, by statute took the status of the mother and is thus born into slavery. The full benefit of the relationship and the off-spring enured to the White male. Under English precedent, the status of children was determined by the father. The colonists changed the law to increase the

wealth and domination of the White master who had eliminated certain costs of purchasing human labor by becoming 'a breeder of slaves.' The Black female, woman or child, was forced into sexual relationships for the White slave master's pleasure and profit."

—*Gloria J. Browne-Marshall, Failing Our Black Children: Statutory Rape Laws, Moral Reform and the Hypocrisy of Denial*

Diabolical. Disturbing. Disgusting. And downright selfishly hateful! That is the core mentality of the White male slave owners and the White women who either sat quietly by or beat their Black women slaves because they were not brave enough to expose their husbands or leave them.

You may be tired of my passionately descriptive expression of the truth, and that's okay. It doesn't change the fact that the truth is the truth. You may also be thinking, *"Not all White people owned slaves or participated in the slave trade or slave labor."* It doesn't matter, so stop using it as a defense or justification for WHAT DID HAPPEN for three-plus centuries. My response to your thought is, *"**So what!** ALL of your people, the generations before you, benefited from slavery in the form of pleasure, political gain, or profit—you included, and you still do today."*

Better thoughts and questions to ask yourself include:

- *Where were White women when African/Black women needed you most?*
- *Why didn't the majority of White women come to our rescue?*

- *Why didn't White women more frequently and aggressively stand up to and fight against the **evil crime against humanity** called slavery?*

- *Why didn't more White women look into the eyes of the slave woman's mulatto children and love them as her own?*

- *Why didn't more White women leave those statutory rapists, aka husbands and slave breeders, and expose them?*

- *Why didn't more White women look into our desperate and dying eyes and see us as human beings instead of **human punching bags** and sinful seducers of their men?*

- *Why? Why? Why?*

The deeply-rooted, systemic, and socially profound conflicts between White women and Black women are real, are often felt but unspoken, and are anchored in EVERYTHING I just shared. And that covers only the centuries before slavery was abolished at the national level. The decades after slavery ended would also prove to be challenging times between White women and Black women, as I touched on in Chapter Six. Then we endured nearly another century more of racial struggle and strife, and it continues today.

White Supremacy and racism are NOT over! **Please stop saying they are.** We are not post-racial, just like we are not post-sexism. And if you want racism and sexism to really be over, **stop being an Antagonist and Advocate and become an Ally in the fight against social and racial injustice.** It started with you, and it will end with you. *True* history teaches that the construct of "race" and all its eventual evils were created by White people. This passage from Audrey Smedley's article, titled "Origin of the Idea of Race," explains:

> *Toward the end of the eighteenth century, the image of Africans began to change dramatically. The major catalyst for this transformation was the rise of a powerful antislavery movement that expanded and strengthened during the Revolutionary Era both in Europe and in the United States. As a consequence, proslavery forces found it necessary to develop new arguments for defending the institution. Focusing on physical differences, they turned to the notion of the natural inferiority of Africans and thus their God-given suitability for slavery. Such arguments became more frequent and strident from the end of the eighteenth century on, and the characterizations of Africans became more negative.*
>
> *From here we see the structuring of the ideological components of "race." The term "race," which had been a classificatory term like "type," or "kind," but with ambiguous meaning, became more widely used in the eighteenth century, and crystallized into a distinct reference for Africans, Indians and Europeans. By focusing on the physical and status differences between the conquered and enslaved peoples, and Europeans, the emerging ideology linked the socio-political status and physical traits together and created a new form of social identity. Proslavery leaders among the colonists formulated a new ideology that merged all Europeans together, rich and poor, and fashioned a social system of ranked physically distinct groups. The model for "race" and "races" was the Great Chain of Being or Scale of Nature (Scala Naturae), a semi-scientific theory of a natural hierarchy of all living things, derived from classical Greek writings. The physical*

features of different groups became markers or symbols of their status on this scale, and thus justified their positions within the social system. Race ideology proclaimed that the social, spiritual, moral, and intellectual inequality of different groups was, like their physical traits, natural, innate, inherited, and unalterable.

Thus was created the only slave system in the world that became exclusively "racial." By limiting perpetual servitude to Africans and their descendants, colonists were proclaiming that blacks would forever be at the bottom of the social hierarchy. By keeping blacks, Indians and whites socially and spatially separated and enforcing endogamous mating, they were making sure that visible physical differences would be preserved as the premier insignia of unequal social statuses. From its inception separateness and inequality was what "race" was all about. The attributes of inferior race status came to be applied to free blacks as well as slaves. In this way, "race" was configured as an autonomous new mechanism of social differentiation that transcended the slave condition and persisted as a form of social identity long after slavery ended.

—Audrey Smedley, "Origin of the Idea of Race," Anthropology Newsletter, November 1997

Racism is not a people of color problem; it's a White people problem, and you are the best solution to ending what you started. People of color have been fighting for centuries to end this *world evil* to no avail; it still persists and plagues the lives of people all over the globe. You and your ancestors may not have owned slaves or participated in the travesty of the American slavery system, yet you and ALL your ancestors have benefited from it. And with an *Awakened Conscious Shift* of your thoughts and behaviors, you can help shut the door on Pandora's box once and for all!

I'm sure you have a lot of questions, would love to make comments to me as you read my words, and/or have so many times wanted to close this book and toss it in the trash. If you're still reading, that's wonderful; I hope you read on, let it soak in, do more research and reading, and then take action to do your part to eradicate racism in the world and to become an Ally for the women of color and Black women in your life. Here's a short list of actions you can take and things to consider if you really want to become a White Ally:

- *Becoming a White Ally is an inside job. If you do not believe you have White Privilege, then you are not ready to become an Ally. Period!* **THIS is the first and most crucial work you must do.**

- *Your primary racial justice work must be done largely with White people. Instead of debating with people of color about anything I've said, turn that conversation toward your own home, community, friends, and family. We don't need you drilling us with thousands of questions, looking for us to educate you, or putting us in a position to explain to you what we've tried to explain too many times to count before.*

- **Stop talking. Stop defending. Stop comparing. Stop justifying. Stop shifting the focus. Stop blaming victims. Just stop!** *Instead, start listening, reading, studying, researching, and putting all this on* repeat for a while until you are more objectively equipped to engage in race talks and begin your racial justice journey.

- Wake up and pay attention to who is missing! Notice who is missing at the tables of decision-makers and policy makers, in leadership roles, on powerful platforms, and all the other spaces and places where the REAL power lies. And even if you see one or a few people of color in those places, that doesn't mean it's time to stop looking.

- Notice when you feel afraid or threatened by Black people, notice when you lock your doors or clutch your purse, notice when you use the words **"those people,"** notice when you feel superior, notice how you feel and what you do when a Black person is in a space where you don't think they belong, notice how many commercials you see that do not include people of color, notice how the media portrays Black people, simply wake up and be conscious of what's happening in the world.

- And lastly, although I provide some basic dos and don'ts for your journey in Chapter Ten, figuring out your journey is your work to do. Be genuine.**Be ready to be uncomfortable, a lot. Be willing to open your version of Pandora's box within your own family.** Chances are that some White person you know will make a racist statement, tell a racist joke, or demonstrate some type of blatant racist behavior. Call them out. Confront them. And this means you must be willing to sever ties with racist people, or at least minimize your contact with them. **This work is for the courageous and brave, and it does NO one any good for you to sit on the fence of Advocacy. You gotta be all in or get all out.**

Instead of asking yourself, *"What does this have to do with me?"* I'd like you to ask yourself questions like these:

- *What if starting today the roles changed, and people of color had the political and financial power to enslave you, your children, and all the White people you know for the next five hundred years just because you have White skin?*

- *What if during the next five centuries White women were raped and beaten by Black men just for the hell of it, including your preteen and teenage daughters, nieces, and granddaughters? What kind of psychological wounds would be endured from century to century?*

- *What if you were forced to pack up and leave your family and become an indentured servant to a Black woman who hates you and a Black man who beats and rapes you whenever he wants, and then you get pregnant and he denies your children?*

- *What if you had to breastfeed Black women's children and barely had enough milk and nourishment for your own babies?*

- *What if you were snatched out of your home right now and forced to go far away to be a slave for the rest of your life, and your name was changed to an African name and your children had to carry that name?*

- *What if Black women had the power to change the current laws and they abolished White women's right to vote, and you had to fight for decades to get your rights back?*

- *What if people of color had the right to enter your home and tell you to get out because they were taking over your land and property, and you and your family were left homeless in your own land?*

- *What if people of color changed roles with all the White people in power today, and societal norms and rules were shaped by the Black woman's and man's perspective, traditions, beliefs, thoughts, and culture? And what if you had to learn how to survive in this environment?*

- *What if the Black woman was the epitome of beauty, the icon and standard of the ideal woman, the woman who every other woman in the world strived to be like? And what if, no matter how hard you tried, you could never measure up to her in society's eyes?*

- *What if, for the next three-hundred-plus years, you were forced to eat scraps, and you were not allowed to be educated, not allowed to own property or pass it on to your children, not allowed to start your own business, and not allowed to be independent of your Black slavemaster? What if you saw your White men being lynched in the streets day after day while Black men stood around and laughed, and what if you had to watch your daughters, nieces, and granddaughters be put up for sale on the auction block for pennies while Black men fantasized about all the nasty, sexual things they could do—at their leisure and with no recourse—to the young women of your family?*

Now again, imagine this happening for three-hundred-plus years, to you, your children, and your family. What state of mind do you think White people would be in? How would White fathers show up in the world as they carried all this anger, pain, and historical wounds around in their spirit? How would White people really and truly feel about Black people having all the power, privileges, and rights for so long with little to no regard for White human life? What kind of relationships would White and

Black women have? And finally, what if almost every Black person you knew said these things to you after all those years of brutal enslavement, the Jim Crow Era, separate but equal laws, church burnings and bombings, the hateful waving of the AFRICAN flag, along with all the other collateral damage caused by the evil roots and seeds of White slavery? What if after ALL that history, and the current racism and oppression, Black people had the insensitive audacity to make one of these statements to you:

- *"Get over it, slavery is over now!"*
- *"I didn't own your people, so don't take it out on me."*
- *"I'm Black but I do not have any special privileges."*
- *"White people have just as much privilege as Black people; stop making excuses."*
- *"There you go again making this a race issue; why do you have to always pull the race card?"*
- *"So explain to me again why you're so upset, and do it nicely, please."*
- *"I'm Colorblind... I don't see color; I just see people."*
- *"Why are you so upset that Black people still fly the African flag? It's just part of our heritage and national pride."*

Mind you, it has not been even sixty years since President Johnson signed the Civil Rights Act of 1964 prohibiting and making it illegal to discriminate based on race, religion, or natural origin. Sixty years! This means "legally" just TWO generations of Black people have been "freed" of racist behaviors, laws, and rules, and that's only on paper. We know racism still happens every day. Let me also add that the first African/Black slave arrived in the

Commonwealth of Virginia in 1619. Yeah, you do the math!

God only knows what all happened to Black people for so many centuries, but one thing is for sure: **their greatest perpetrator, rapist, pedophile, and murderer has been White people.** Now you tell me with a straight face, and with heart-felt sincerity spoken in truth, that YOU have not benefited from the evils of slavery and White Privilege. That you **do not** benefit from three-hundred-plus years of history and legacy of White power, economic power, political domination, social prestige, religious preference, laws, rules, standards, and governance. After all, many of the founding fathers supported slavery and/or owned slaves themselves.

Come on... **Wake UP! It's a hard pill to swallow, but you must, immediately.** And if you don't, that's cool too, but for the sake of humanity, I hope you do, and I hope you then get busy becoming an Ally in the fight for social and racial justice for all! It's also significantly important to note that **you should NOT self-appoint yourself an Ally; the title of "Ally" is one that must be earned, and it is bestowed by people of color to White people.** Nope! That's one thing your privilege cannot buy. You just can't TAKE that title just because you've read a few books, taken a few classes, or have begun your anti-racism work. To appoint yourself an Ally is disrespectful and invalid.

Ladies, the world is in dire need of our help and intervention! We *are* the beings of love, compassion, forgiveness, nurturance, and communication. We have been divinely endowed with the gifts, talents, skills, and sense of community-building to be the Western woman, no matter what part of the world we live in. We are the women who will heal, change, and transform the world, but it won't happen until we begin to heal and save ourselves as a gender first. We will not fully carry out this desperately needed mission until we say NO MORE to *Cliques, Catfights* and *Colorblindness*. It will be our differences that allow us to dismantle systems that destroy communities because of race, and to dig up the ravenous roots that create social and racial injustices for people everywhere. **It's time for a wake-up call! It's time for an Awakened Conscious Shift!**

WAKE-UP CALL QUESTIONS

Does it really make a difference that you or your family "did not own slaves?" Why is it so difficult for you to just believe and speak the truth about American slavery?

_____

_____

_____

_____

_____

_____

If the roles were reversed and you and your family had to trade places with Black people now and for generations past, how might you feel about Black people, Black women, today?

_____

_____

_____

_____

_____

_____

_____

What will you do to become an Ally for women of color and Black women?

_____

_____

_____

_____

_____

What are you teaching your daughters about privilege and racism?

_____

_____

_____

_____

_____

What do you think will happen within the feminist movement if you DON'T step up and become an Ally?

_____

_____

_____

_____

_____

"Colorblindness is for cowards who don't want to talk about race, and for people who'd rather you deny your identity to keep them comfortable and guilt-free."

CATRICE M. JACKSON

Chapter 9

CLIQUES, CATFIGHTS, AND COLORBLINDNESS

"I can promise you that women working together—
linked, informed and educated—can bring peace and
prosperity to this forsaken planet."

—Isabel Allende

WAKE... UP! Nothing comes to sleepers but a dream. From a literal perspective, a dream does not become a reality until you implement beliefs, thoughts, behaviors, habits, and actions to breathe life into it. We can sit back and dream of a better world to include social and racial equality for women all day long, but until we *do something*, it will remain a dream embedded in our imagination. We all sit back and talk about the ills, evils, disparities, and injustices in the world, but rarely do we get actively involved in doing something to change and transform the world. People are crying out from all corners of the globe, begging for help, deliverance, liberation, and freedom. Every city, state, and country is attempting to deal with eruptions of social, political, and racial unrest. The world needs you and me, and it needs us right now, not tomorrow, but in this very moment that you are reading these words. There's work to be done. **I believe that WOMEN *will* save the world, but NOT unless we save ourselves first.**

The *mysterious* Western woman I tried to define in Chapter Two is no longer a mystery. *She is you. She is me.* She is us. And I don't believe she is ONLY a Western woman. I believe she is a Northern woman. She is a Southern woman. She is an Eastern woman. She is every woman, everywhere. I believe that Western women *will* lead the way but will not, should not, and cannot do it alone. The world belongs to all of us, and we must all be responsible for saving mother earth. **It is our duty, our responsibility, and it must be our joy.** I can tell you three things that must end so we can help, change, and transform the world: *Cliques, Catfights,* and *Colorblindness.* In my opinion, they are the three most unproductive forms of engagement that will continue to divide and conquer us as women.

Cliques, cliques, and more cliques! They begin as early as preschool, and for some women, they last a lifetime. I've participated in them and been the victim of them over my lifetime. Mean, nasty, hateful groups of women can wreak havoc in your life like no one else. In Chapter One, I shared a brief part of my *schoolgirl games* story to show how girls can be so mean and unsupportive of one another. I wish I could say those games end after high school, but unfortunately, many women are still showing up on the playground of life excluding other women, ignoring their greatness, and refusing to support them. What is this about? Why must women engage this way? **Life is not a popularity contest!** We've come a long way, Baby, but we've got an even longer way to go!

It's been said that your network determines the value of

your net worth! Are you stepping outside of your comfort zone to network with women who do not look like you? Are there conscious and unconscious "cliques" in your networking mindset or strategy? Whether in person or online, networking is critical for success in the 21st century. And it's more about *who* you know (or who knows you!) than *what* you know. I wonder if women network differently than men do, and if people of color network differently than White people do. It's my hope that women are learning how to better support other women as they network. I also wonder whether networking among women still has elements of competition and envy, or have women moved beyond internalized sexism. Internalized sexism often causes women to hurt, ridicule, and/or passively decline to support other women for fear those other women will get ahead at a faster pace. Unfortunately, I have seen this happen far too often. So, what is it about women who feel threatened by other strong, ambitious women? That is the million-dollar question!

One of my personal theories is that once a woman "arrives" in a high position (especially if they are the only one, or one of a few, at the top), they fear that another woman will take the spotlight. I also think some women may have low self-esteem and put great value on their "title or position" instead of what is in their heart and soul, and therefore, become very protective of this "place in life or business." If this title or position is compromised, it can be very threatening to a woman who identifies herself by material things and credentials.

Does race compound the situation more? Do Black women have greater difficulty networking with and supporting other Black women, especially if they are alone at the top? Do Latinas have this problem? I realize these are general questions, so there is plenty of room for discrepancy; however, an important question is, *"How can women learn to be more supportive of each other?"* and an even more important question is, *"How can women in power positions learn to support other powerful women?"* It's critical that we don't shut other women out, and that we learn to support other women regardless of race. If we could learn to put our energies into building a collective female force, we could accomplish so much more, as individuals and as a group.

Here are some truths to consider:

- *When a woman is truly confident in her abilities, she doesn't need to worry about another woman stealing her shine.*
- *There are enough opportunities, clients, and business for all women.*
- *If you create and master your personal and professional niches, you'll find that no one else can do what you do like you do it.*
- *Put time into connecting with other women who are like-minded, confident, and genuinely sincere about helping you shine.*
- *You don't need to be afraid of connecting with and supporting another powerful woman; can you imagine the things the two of you could do with that much power and influence?*
- *If you meet a woman who is passionate about her work, and if you lend a hand, share your resources, and help make her dreams a reality, I guarantee that what you give will return to you a hundredfold.*
- *Identify early on in relationships who is really "for" you*

*and "against" you, and give your emotional energy only
to women who support your vision for your life and lift
you up. Ideally, we want to get along with and collaborate
with all women, but many times that's not possible, and
it's okay.*

The power of networking is priceless! When one woman is successful, we all are. Make a concerted effort to support the women in your lives, networks, and communities. **Don't be intimidated by a powerful woman; connect with her and learn from her wisdom and success!** And lastly, stop being Colorblind. Step outside of your comfort zone to intentionally connect with and support women who do not look like you, women of color. Embrace the differences that diversity brings.

Let me tell you a little bit about my journey. It's amazing the support, guidance, and mentorship I received during my eight years as an entrepreneur. Women from diverse backgrounds came to my aid, offered to help, listened to my story, and walked with me on this journey of freedom and personal power. When I stepped out in faith to live my dream of entrepreneurship, I thought a "certain" kind of woman would be right there with me. I just knew that woman X, Y, or Z would be willing to help along the way. Boy, was I surprised. Then reality set in. I needed to diversify my circle of influence, wisdom, and support. I needed to step outside of what I knew and what was most comfortable; I needed to reach out to people who were genuinely interested in helping other women live their dreams.

I even took huge steps to reach out to women who seemed unreachable, and what a wonderful surprise it was to see them embrace my vision. I share my story with all authenticity, because it is important that we do not fear asking for help from women who don't look like us. We must look beyond what is right in front of us and see the possibilities even when they cannot be clearly identified. We have to be willing to believe that women from diverse backgrounds have a tremendous amount of value, and that they will help us manifest our desires, dreams, and purpose. Women of all ages, races, and geographic locations are seeking to be inspired and empowered, and they need your help and mine. I have recommitted to consistently displaying the aura of acceptance. An aura that lets every woman know I am reachable no matter who she is, what she looks like, or where she lives. There is great power in diversifying your circle of influence, wisdom, and support. There is great spiritual reward in creating an aura that speaks to the souls of people and embraces them despite what they look like. As I continue to diversify my circle, I eagerly await the opportunities to engage with fabulous women from all walks of life.

Here are a few suggestions on how to diversify your circle:

- *Seek to add women who are smarter than you, and learn from their wisdom.*
- *Seek to add women who are more financially prosperous than you, and learn how to create your own prosperity.*
- *Seek to add women who look different from you, and become enlightened by their cultural experiences.*
- *Seek to add women who are on lower rungs of the ladder than you are; give back to the world by mentoring other women.*
- *Seek to add women who are fully living the dream, and be inspired by them to live your dreams.*

I've had wonderful opportunities to meet women from a

variety of cultural and ethnic backgrounds in my lifetime, and I feel blessed by those experiences. When we think of "diversity," we may think of the word "different," and we may think "different" means "strange." **No, "different" just means "different," not "weird," "negative," "wrong," or "better."** I believe that to be successful in our lives and careers, we must become culturally intelligent and proficient.

Culture is important in understanding how people think and behave, but in my opinion, it does not get the attention it deserves. I would like to see more psychological research done related to cultural intelligence and the benefit of mastering cognitive-behavioral skills in this area. The United States is such a diverse country; although learning about the various cultures that exist in America (and the world) can be overwhelming, it is necessary to sensitively engage with different people. **We've got global work to do, and we must be educated and equipped to deal with the global challenges facing all women.** Failure to become educated and proficient in cultural issues opens the door for people to be harmed and oppressed by ignorance.

Cultural intelligence is an essential skill set for those who want to be successful in their lives and careers, especially those who work with people and in the human services field. The word "diversity" has become the buzz word of this decade, and while diversity is important, we must now begin to focus on creating inclusivity in workplaces, communities, organizations, and all other American and global systems. Cultural competency is also a relatively new phenomenon, and I would say we need to go beyond competency toward proficiency.

Cultural proficiency is a necessary part of our everyday encounters with people, no matter what line of work we are in. Cultural *competency* is the equivalent to an English-speaking person "trying out" their bilingual skills, whereas Cultural *proficiency* is the ability to speak a second language fluently. When you try out your new language skills, the potential to make mistakes, and hurt, offend, and piss people off is very high, but once you master that language and become fluent, conversations become clearer, fewer mistakes are made, and mutual understanding occurs. **And what is especially important for YOU to know, White women, is that the bulk of YOUR racial justice work will be spent examining your own history and culture, including how White Privilege has shaped and defined the perspectives you have about people of color and how you engage with them.** Notice I said "racial justice work," not cultural competency or proficiency. There's a HUGE difference.

Becoming culturally intelligent allows us to use alternate ways of perceiving the world and the different people in it. I believe it is our perceptions that drive how we respond to people and events. **When we perceive differences as negative things, those perceptions create misunderstandings and prevent us from experiencing the beauty, value, and richness of diversity.** As America and the world increasingly become more diverse, we must become more culturally intelligent, especially in business transactions and employee relations. Cultural intelligence allows individuals to engage with diverse teams and in different cultural settings with more ease, resulting in greater personal and professional respect and relationship success. The ability to relate well to others is vital for creating and maintaining effective organizational teams and business partnerships. A critical first step is for you to drop the belief that Colorblindness is a great personal asset to have. It is not.

Colorblindness is not a good thing! You'll hear varying opinions about that statement, but let me offer you some insight about why I agree with it. I believe one of the first steps toward gaining cultural intelligence is to examine one's own culture and how it shapes who we are. Understanding, valuing, appreciating, and celebrating our own culture allows us to see the value in other people's cultures. Furthermore, it allows us to perceive people as just different, rather than strange or negative. I use cultural intelligence in every encounter with people, even if we are the same race. Cultural identity, values, and beliefs shape who we are, and if people could stop and really see the person in front of them and engage from that perspective, human relations would significantly improve.

We must slow down and see people for who they are, respect their culture, attempt to understand it, and learn from each human encounter with the ultimate goal of becoming culturally wise. When you are Colorblind, you miss out on all the wonderful history and value a person brings to the table, the conversation, and the world. When you are Colorblind, you miss out on the struggles and strife that have shaped people into who they've become. Every piece of who we are matters, but when you are Colorblind, you miss pieces of a person's soul puzzle. Although our differences often cause us pain, they are also what makes us beautiful and unique.

Colorblindness *especially* creates chaos in relationships between Black and White women. Many White women wear their Colorblindness like a badge of honor. They are so proud to proclaim their Colorblindness. While you'll find many women of color who do NOT want you to see the color of their skin, there are just as many, if not more, who do want YOU to SEE it. **Not to be treated differently because of it, but for you to see, recognize, honor, respect, appreciate, and value the experiences that come from living in their Black or brown skins.**

So, what happens when you engage with a Black woman while proudly wearing your Colorblindness badge of honor? Probably nothing much if you engage on a very superficial level although a cultural collision is possible; almost certainly a cultural collision at the crossroads of Intersectionality if the discussion or engagement goes deeper. I bet many Black women are like me: *they've experienced more racism and oppression from White women than from any other group of people.* If you don't understand why, you haven't absorbed the messages in this book thus far. I suggest you go back and re-read the previous chapters, and research the history of Black and White women. The best advice I can give you is to **take off that Colorblindness badge of honor, and NEVER put it on again.**

Cultural proficiency requires you to step outside of your White Picket Fence and go into the communities and neighborhoods that are different from your own. **Be careful how you enter, though!** The best way to learn is from (not about) various cultures of people without being invasive, offensive, and expecting them to educate you. It's highly inappropriate and offensive to ASK people of color to explain their plight and struggles to you. Even when they offer to explain or share, tread lightly! The best and most respectful and effective thing you can do is listen. Don't listen to respond or to ask a thousand, inappropriate questions; instead, listen with the intent to hear their stories, pain, and struggles. **Your role is not to justify, blame, shift the focus onto you, minimize, deny, and/or question what they've shared. Your role is to LISTEN and then do your own research on what YOU can do to honor their experiences and truths, and to avoid being an Antagonist in their lives.**

This is where many White women get it all wrong. Becoming culturally proficient is not about "them"; it's about you and what you are responsible for knowing and doing to respect and honor their differences, their culture. Racial justice work is one hundred percent about you and how you will begin to use your White Privilege to end racism and foster social and racial justice for people of color. I suggest you start your racial justice work in your heart, mind, and soul, and then move from there to your home, children, neighborhood, and community, and then out into the world.

A great place to start is by assessing your degree of personal diversity. The word "diversity" often leads us to think of race, ethnicity, gender, age, and/or religion, but there is so much more to it. No matter how you define it, diversity is a beautiful mosaic that creates an essence of richness in the world. Everyone has a story, a story that should be heard, valued, and respected. While I realize that women of different ethnicities face different challenges, all women have a common bond called "womanhood." It is at that bond where we must connect to fully understand the individual and cultural differences that make up the beautiful mosaic. **How diverse is your circle?**

- *Do you have friends of different races?*
- *Are your clients from various racial and ethnic backgrounds?*
- *Do you have women of color on your teams, committees, or boards?*
- *How many business partnerships or collaborations have included aligning with a woman of color?*
- *Do your magazine covers feature women of different races?*
- *When you select speakers for your events, are you intentionally seeking out women of color because you honor their brilliance and contributions?*

- *When you host an event, do most of the participants look like you, or is it a beautiful mosaic of different shades of women?*
- *Does your marketing plan specifically include strategies to attract more women of color to your business, programs, and/or organization?*
- *Do you consciously make the effort to hire and promote women of color and Black women?*

These are essential questions to ask yourself. If the answers are not all YES, you've got some work to do. As the *"browning of America"* continues to evolve, many folks believe that one day everyone will be a shade of brown. It is estimated that by the year 2050, White people will no longer be the majority in the U.S. If this is true, it means your boss may be a person of color one day, if they are not already. This means you may encounter more people who do not look like you, think like you, and/or speak like you. This means your grandchildren may be biracial or multiracial. **Hopefully, this means that White Supremacy will be taking its last breath into a long-awaited death!**

Change is coming. Change is happening right now. Are you prepared to engage with different people in different settings? Start now by making connections with as many "different" people as possible. Not just any connections, but deep, genuine, and respectful alliances with women of color. As you open up new relationships with women of color and Black women, lose the **"I don't see color" phraseology and all forms of it.** Simply put, "to be Colorblind" is to be ignorant, in denial, and/or to minimize the experiences of people of color. Yes, people of color want to be treated like everyone else; however, their experiences in life and their ancestors' legacies are pieces of their story that cannot be denied. To see color means to see a critical part of that person's life experiences. Besides, color is beautiful... look at it, see it, acknowledge it, embrace it, and just accept that it exists.

What kind of culturally proficient legacy will you leave to your children and grandchildren? Start talking to your kids about differences, privilege, racism, and inclusion. Teach them to not be afraid of someone who does not look like them. Allow them to experience the flavor of differences; it will enrich their lives and create new generations of inclusion. Inclusion will become a daily way of being instead of an agenda item, policy, or procedure. And finally, make a commitment to NOT engage in paper cuts (aka racial microaggressions)! As I discussed in Chapter Three, microaggressions are like paper cuts and mosquito bites: small yet painful and annoying injuries if you get just one, unbearable as they add up in a day and over a lifetime. I have already shared many of the ways you inflict paper cuts to people who are different from you, and I have provided a resource list at the end of this book so you can do more of your own research.

Now let's address Catfights! There is a little princess in all of us, and there is a full-grown woman as well. The little princess is our "girl" self who sometimes overshadows the full-grown woman and can lead to our own demise. When these two parts of us are not aligned, we are living out of balance. Let's talk about the little girl or princess who lives within us as women. She is often immature, self-centered, envious, catty, controlling, whiny, and insecure. Think back to your adolescent days of middle and high school. Can you recall the cliques and how girls betrayed, preyed upon, and ostracized other girls? As I wrote in my book *Delicious! The Savvy Woman's Guide to Living a Sweet, Sassy and Satisfied Life:*

I too once was involved in those types of shenanigans and recall the pain and misery I felt and caused on occasion.

Those were moments of transformation as we tried to figure out who we were and where we stood in the world of other people and especially other females. I remember judging other girls by how they looked, what they did, and who they hung out with, and knowing that I too was under that same social microscope. Although I was generally pretty authentic and a leader versus a follower, I too fell victim to and perpetrator of the "mean girl" syndrome. Through my personal transformation, I realized there is no place for the little princess or the mean girl syndrome in my life. Yet, as you may have discovered, there are plenty of grown (in age) women who still allow this way of living and engaging to permeate their lives.

Let me back up and explain what I mean by girl versus woman. Think back to your middle school and high school days. You can probably recall incidents when you or other girls participated in the "mean girl" games. You know what I am talking about: the gossiping, snickering, leaving certain girls out, judging and classifying other girls, cliques against cliques, and so on. I believe we all know and have either been the victim or perpetrator in these types of games. Now, think about how the victims must have felt and how nasty and emotionally draining this type of behavior was. Those were girl behaviors. At this point in your life, ideally you have graduated from the school of girlhood and emerged as a full-grown, whole woman.

Unlike a girl, a woman is confident in her own skin. She's satisfied with who she is, no matter what titles and credentials she does or does not hold. She doesn't take everything personally, knows her core values and lives by them, and treats others with kindness and respect. What another woman wears, what she looks like, and whether she is pretty or not does NOT matter to a woman, because a woman sees the souls of other women not their outward definitions. I could continue, but you get the picture. A woman does not play those schoolgirl games. These "mean girl" games continue to show up in our lives and careers today. If you've recently said or thought "Who does she think she is?" You may still have traces of "girl" flowing through your veins. The little princess (girl) inside wants all the attention, gets emotional when things don't go her way, pouts and maybe even cries at the drop of a hat, thinks the world should revolve around her, etc. The little princess wants the best Barbie, has to be the mommy or teacher when playing games, gets jealous when her friends play with other friends—and the scenarios continue. Okay, now for the point of all this: Who wants to be around someone like the little princess? Who wants to hire or promote her? Who wants to date her? Who wants to be on her team? I may be going out on a limb here, but I would say "No one!"

The little princess in you still functions from a place of insecurity and false feelings of superiority. On rare occasions she shows up in my life; however, I have intentionally told her to go take a hike and get out of my way so the whole, full-grown, mature woman in me can reign. Yes, in my Queendom, there is absolutely no room for the little princess—only the queen diva (Divine, Inspirational, Vibrant, and Aspiring) sister in me rules my space. What I know to be true is that the little princess causes many women to live an incongruent life. The little princess is alive and kicking on the inside, yet often women will try to portray something else to the world. A full-grown woman—a savvy woman—lives in balance and has declared dominion over her Queendom with no tolerance for the little princess' existence.

What I know for sure is that the little princess has or does live in all women despite race or ethnicity. If we as women are going to truly master "supporting one another," we must tell the little princess to take a hike so the full-grown woman can emerge and soar! I encourage you to check yourself to see if the little princess is reigning in your life and how she may be not only impacting and damaging your relationships with other women but your relationships in general.

—Catrice M. Jackson, Delicious! The Savvy Woman's Guide to Living a Sweet, Sassy and Satisfied Life

Cliques, Catfights, and *Colorblindness* will keep us stuck, stagnant, and in survival mode, and you and I deserve better than that. The world needs us now! We don't have time to be excluding one another, fighting one another, discriminating against and oppressing one another, and denying and ignoring the beauty and brilliance of one another. **I believe that WOMEN *will* save the world, but NOT unless we save ourselves first.** Every single woman on the planet, not just the "Western" woman, must WAKE UP to what's happening around us, and we must actively and relentlessly do our part in healing, restoring, and transforming the world. You've got work to do, and so do I.

It would be naive to believe that you will LIKE every woman you encounter, but I do believe it is possible to respect every woman you meet by seeing her for who she is, skin color and culture included. At any given moment, you and I are playing the role of *Antagonist, Advocate,* or *Ally* while connecting and engaging with other women. Regardless of our racial, cultural, and socioeconomic differences, the definitions of Antagonist, Advocate, and Ally apply. And in every moment, you have the power to choose to step out of a "role" and be an Ally for every woman you encounter. Madeleine Albright, the first female United States Secretary of State, says it best: *"There is a special place in hell for women who don't help other women."* I'll add to her statement by leaving you with this: *"Be an Ally or have a safe trip!"*

WAKE-UP CALL QUESTIONS

Now that you know that Colorblindness creates collateral damage, how much damage have you caused in the lives of women of color and Black women, and what will you do differently?

_____

_____

_____

_____

_____

Where in your life, work, or ministry are you still "cat fighting" with other women, and why?

_____

_____

_____

_____

_____

_____

How are you excluding other women from your life, events, programs, and groups, and why?

_____

_____

_____

_____

_____

How will you do YOUR part to heal and save the world?

_____

_____

_____

_____

_____

How will you use your White Privilege to break down barriers between women and to fight for social and racial justice?

_____

_____

_____

_____

_____

Chapter 10

CLIQUES, CATFIGHTS, AND COLORBLINDNESS

"I've learned that people will forget what you said, people will forget what you did, but people will never forget how you made them feel."

—*Maya Angelou*

If you've made it to this part of the book, I have a strong feeling that you desire to become an Ally in the lives of women of color and Black women. There's so much for you to learn and do, and as overwhelming as it is, you must do it. I'll share five behaviors for you to avoid and five important actions to take to help you get started. This information may sound like much of what you've already learned from this book. But it is worth repeating and rephrasing so you begin to see the importance of how to stop oppressing other women, women of color, and Black women. These lists are not exhaustive, but they are significant starting places.

Here are the five things you should ***not*** do:

1. DO NOT BECOME A SELF-TITLED ALLY.

Before you start shouting *"I am an Ally"* from the mountaintop, please know *this* and **don't forget it**: You do not give yourself the title of White Ally. That title is given to you only by people of color! The giving of such a title is similar to the concept of *"respect is earned, not given."* You must earn the title, and not by what you say, but by who you are and how you genuinely and consistently show up on the battlefield of racial justice. You can call yourself whatever you want, but unless people of color deem you an Ally, don't flaunt that word around. If you do, expect to be called out about it, and don't get offended, because I've warned you!

2. DON'T TRY TO TELL WOMEN OF COLOR AND BLACK WOMEN THAT YOU UNDERSTAND WHAT THEY ARE FEELING, AND DON'T ATTEMPT TO SPEAK FOR THEM.

There is no man in this world who truly knows what it is like to be a woman. Men may be sensitive to the challenges that women face and feel a sense of empathy, but because they are men, they are not fully capable of deeply understanding women's issues. Therefore, they simply cannot speak for women. At best, they can speak up on *behalf* of women as allies to end sexism in all its forms. The same is true for White women. While all women may share similar struggles around class, religion, gender, and/or socioeconomic status, White women cannot deeply understand what it means to live and breathe in Black or brown skin. Avoid the temptation to put yourself in a woman of color's shoes when it comes to race and ethnicity. Instead, listen without judgment. Don't question her reality. **Don't ask her to prove her experience. Don't shift the focus onto yourself.** These types of behaviors are counterproductive and essentially disempower her.

You'll notice this book was NOT filled with a lot of research and statistics. That was done purposely. I've shared my personal truths as well as the stories and truths of the many women of color and Black women who've crossed my path. If you want proof, open up your eyes and SEE what is happening in the lives of women of color and Black women, and if that isn't enough, there are plenty of resources and information for you to seek out, and you can come to your own conclusions. That's your work to do. **And if I'm brutally honest, women of color and Black women are tired of trying to prove to you and the world that we matter, that we are worthy, and that the pain of our oppression and struggle is REAL.**

3. DON'T LEAD, FOLLOW—UNLESS YOU'RE LEADING WHITE PEOPLE.

In the fight for social and racial justice, White Allies always stand alongside people of color, never in front of them. Whenever you feel the urge to step in front of people of color on the battlefield, remind yourself that you are **misusing your power**. I'm sure you'd appreciate men taking a stand for women's rights, but I don't think you'd like them to become the spokesmen leading the way and speaking for you. You're quite capable of speaking for yourself, right? Same theory applies with race. Who knows better than women of color and Black women what our challenges and struggles are, and what we need, want, and desire? The best option is for you to become a leader and voice for White people who are against racism and fighting to eliminate it. **Your greatest work will consist of you doing your own personal work and then rallying like-minded White people to stand with you as you stand with us.**

4. DON'T THINK YOU'VE MASTERED BEING AN ALLY. THE WORK IS NEVER DONE UNTIL YOU TAKE YOUR LAST BREATH.

I don't believe I will see the elimination of racism in my lifetime, but I DO KNOW I'll take my last breath fighting for social and racial justice by any means necessary. If I don't, my children and my children's children will never be free from the oppressive grip of White Supremacy. **If you DON'T keep fighting until you take your last breath, your children and your children's children will harm my children and my children's children, and my children will literally die, or die inside from a million paper cuts, just because of their skin color.** WE owe it to humanity and future generations to fight a good fight even when we are weary and want to give up. I can't imagine that you would want your children and grandchildren to intentionally or unintentionally hurt other people, to kill them literally or figuratively. That's exactly what will happen if YOU don't commit today to doing your work to eliminate racism.

When you find yourself exhausted, overwhelmed, stressed, or angry while on the journey to end racism, stop and think about how women of color and Black women are a thousand times more exhausted, overwhelmed, stressed, and angry. **You have the luxury of quitting; we don't.** White Privilege gives you that free pass. I hope you take your free pass, burn it, and never look back. You'll never know it all. You'll never read enough books or articles. You'll never have too many race talks. You'll never "get it" completely. The elimination of racism may never happen. You and I may never experience a racism-free world, but we MUST give it one hell of a shot... until we take our last breaths.

5. DON'T EXPECT OR ASK WOMEN OF COLOR AND BLACK WOMEN TO DISCUSS RACE ISSUES WITH YOU IN A "NICE" WAY TO MAKE YOU COMFORTABLE.

Maybe you've heard of the *"Angry Black Woman."* Maybe you've used the terminology yourself; maybe you've wondered, *"Why are Black women so angry?"* Not **all** Black women are angry, but now that you've read this book, I hope you see why they might be. You may have even thought that *I'm* angry as you've read this book. Honestly, sometimes I am angry about the racial injustices in the world and the personal racist attacks I experience, but I'm mostly passionate about fostering justice and quality of life for all people.

Have you ever heard a man say something like, *"Women who talk passionately about feminism are bitchy"*? When you encounter men who just don't understand why women want equal rights, do you speak "nicely" about your rationale, or do you get fired up in your belly and speak with passion and sometimes anger? **Don't you get sick and tired of men minimizing the struggles of women?** Don't you get pissed off when men give you ridiculous rationales about why women are not treated equally? If you are a passionate feminist or women's empowerment advocate, would you be offended and pissed off if men expected you to talk nicely about the marginalization and oppression of women?

First of all, to expect "niceness" from women of color and Black women during race talks is a byproduct of your White Privilege. Second, it's offensive! Men expect you to not get upset as a byproduct of their male privilege, and that's offensive too. And the expectation of niceness further oppresses the oppressed. **When you expect women of color and Black women to be nice during race talks, your White Fragility is rearing its ugly head, and you are indeed operating in a racist way.** On your journey toward Allyship, one of your biggest challenges will be to turn in your White Fragility card and never seek to get it back.

Please STOP all these behaviors now! Cease from further oppressing women of color and Black women with your White Fragility. The road toward Allyship will challenge you in ways you can never imagine. The brutal truth is either you remain an Antagonist or you become an Ally, because straddling the fence as an Advocate is dangerous and lethal.

Here are the five things you *should* do to help you start your journey toward Allyship:

1. TELL YOURSELF THE DAMN TRUTH.

This step is highly critical! The truth will surely set you free. By any means necessary, you're going to need to dig deep into your conscious and unconscious beliefs about women of color and Black women. You're human just like me, and you're also imperfect just like me. Essentially, you have some deep-seated beliefs and judgments about women of color and Black women. **And to say you don't is a lie.** I won't go into why I believe this, because what's more important is for you to tell the truth. If you have a desire to become an Ally for Black women, you've got to release the skeletons from your closet. You've got to take the time to sit down and ask yourself—with no filters—what thoughts, beliefs, stereotypes, and judgments you have about Black women. It's been said that *"What's in your heart comes out of your mouth."* How do you feel in your heart about Black women?

Here's a simple exercise. Take out a sheet of paper and write, "Black women are_____." And then just let it flow! The writing should be spontaneous and uncensored. In other words, be sure to write the exact words that come to mind without trying to alter them and without allowing guilt or shame to censor your writing. Just do it! You don't have to tell anyone what you write. This truth is for you, and it will set you free. Yes, I am asking you to generalize. That's what racism is all about: the generalizations of one race projected onto another, and the mistreatment of the "other race" because of those stereotypes. After you complete the writing, take a long look at your responses, and then dig for a deeper level of truth by asking yourself these follow-up questions:

- *Why did I write these responses?*
- *Where did my beliefs come from; how did I learn them?*
- *Do I really believe these things about Black women?*
- **Why** *do I believe these things about Black women?*
- *Are my beliefs about Black women true?*

If you don't tell yourself the truth about what's deep in your heart and mind, your negative thoughts and beliefs will emerge in one way or another in how you behave toward Black women, to their face and behind their back. Tell yourself *your truths*, and then begin doing your own personal work to dispel the myths, eliminate the stereotypes, and begin to see Black women with new eyes. If you are unwilling to do this first step, you are certainly an Antagonist, and we will SEE you as one regardless of what you say. We don't want to hear you say, *"I'm not racist."* **We want you to show us that you are courageously using your White Privilege to dismantle the evil, deadly, and often invisible system of racism.**

2. OWN YOUR WHITE PRIVILEGE.

You are a White Privileged woman. Period. The best thing you can do to help eliminate racism and empower your Black and brown sisters is to accept and own that truth. Sure, you didn't ask to be born White, just as I didn't ask to be born Black. Therefore, we have to own the skin we are in and accept the benefits and consequences that come with it. Failing to own your White Privilege will certainly create collateral damage in your relationships with women of color and Black women, whether it's intentional or not. **The acceptance of your privilege is your greatest work to do.**

After telling yourself the truth, the owning of your White Privilege will be the most powerful and transformational personal contribution you can make to the feminist empowerment movement and the elimination of racism. If you are struggling with this, I suggest you connect with other White people, particularly White women, who have already crossed this bridge. I realize that no matter how often I say you are privileged because you are White, you may not believe it. You need to hear this truth and the reasons why it's true from other White people. Once you realize it and own it, then it's time for you to use it for good. You must use your privilege and power to challenge, call out, and address other White people who have yet to cross the bridge of ownership and help them along. If you refuse to own it, you are indeed an Antagonist.

3. DO YOUR OWN PERSONAL WORK.

There is no doubt that the journey toward Allyship will stretch you, frustrate you, piss you off, anger you, drain you, and overwhelm you. Buckle up and get ready for one hell of a ride! From this point on, don't ever ask or expect women of color and Black women to educate you about racism. That class is no longer being offered. **This is your work, and you must**

take the lead. The information available to you about racism, oppression, and White Privilege is limitless, so there is no excuse for NOT knowing. **Ignorance is not bliss; it's dangerous. It's time to commit!**

- *Make the commitment to start with you, your home, your children, and within your intimate relationships.*
- *Make the commitment to bring your unconscious bias and racism forward, and make them conscious so you can do something about them.*
- *Make the commitment to stop making excuses for not knowing, and become informed.*
- *Make the commitment to turn in your White Fragility card, and never ask for it back.*
- *Make the commitment to consciously engage with women of color and Black women by SEEING color and honoring the truth that comes with it.*
- *Make the commitment to stop inflicting paper cuts (microaggressions) onto women of color and Black women).*
- *Make the commitment to refrain from denying, questioning, and minimizing the truths and experiences of women of color and Black women.*
- *Make the commitment to stand when you feel like running. To keep going when you are angry, frustrated, and overwhelmed. To boldly call out racism when you see or hear it, even in your family and with your friends.*
- *Make the commitment to stop misappropriating the cultures of people of color.*

- *Make the commitment to understand Intersectionality and engage consciously to avoid causing collateral damage at the intersection of gender and race.*

- *Make the commitment to stop saying you empower ALL women if you really don't, don't know how, refuse to own your White Privilege, and/or refuse to become an Ally.*

- *Make the commitment to commit!*

4. BE MORE CONSCIOUS, INTENTIONAL, AND INCLUSIVE.

Words come a dime a dozen and actions speak louder than words. You may be able to fool people with the words you say, but how you show up will always express the truth. The brand of YOU is at risk. **Your personal and professional brand is at risk.** What I am about to share next is specifically for leaders of women's organizations, women in leadership positions, female coaches who coach other women, entrepreneurs and business owners whose clients are predominantly women, feminist empowerment activists, and any women who teaches, serves, counsels, coaches, leads, or mentors other women. **Today is the day you stop telling lies and hiding behind the facade of the generic umbrella of "empowering women."**

If you, for example, market and/or promote a business or service that caters to women, you must become more consciously inclusive. You can say you're inclusive and invite all women to play and participate, but the *truth* will be revealed in many ways. Answer the following questions to discover exactly how conscious, intentional, and inclusive you really are:

- *How racially diverse are the women you have personal friendships with?*

- *How racially diverse is your professional team?*

- *How racially diverse are the clients you serve?*
- *How racially diverse are the partners you collaborate with?*
- *How racially diverse are the women who sign up for your programs and/or attend your events?*
- *How racially diverse are your social media friends and contacts?*
- *How racially diverse are the networking and social events you attend?*
- *How racially diverse are the people you invite to collaborate with, speak at your events, and/or partner with?*
- *How racially diverse are the women you support and buy from?*
- *How racially diverse are the women you refer business to?*
- *How racially diverse are the women on the covers of your magazines, or the women you highlight in your work?*
- *Do you consciously and intentionally reach out to, invite to play, partner with, support, recognize, refer to, and buy from women of color and Black women?*

Your answers to these questions will reveal just how conscious and intentional you really are. If in every part of your life and career the women you see and engage with look like you, there's a problem. **And if this is true, please STOP saying that you support, work with, and empower ALL women, because it is a LIE, and we SEE the lies.** For us, the lies are a sign of dishonesty, and dishonesty negatively affects your integrity, and weak integrity breaks down your credibility, and poor credibility damages your brand. What's most important for you to know is that while you're hiding behind the facade of empowering all women, women of color and Black women see HOW you are showing up. They see the truth.

If women of color and Black women are not showing up to your events, joining your teams, networking with you, hanging out with you, partnering with you, and/or utilizing your services, there is a reason. **The reason is you have NOT made it a point to be consciously and intentionally inclusive.** You have not invited them to play, participate, or partner with you. Your communication and/or marketing message is not speaking to them, and most importantly, how you are showing up says to them, *"You're not welcome."* You can continue to broadcast that message in your brand and marketing, or you can **WAKE UP, be intentional, and walk your talk.** It's not enough to say you empower ALL women. You've got to *actually do it,* and not just for the sake of saying that you did. Lastly, oh yes! WE women of color and Black women notice all of the above, and we are definitely talking about it when you think we are not. Being unconscious and exclusive is brand suicide!

5. START NOW AND EXPECT TO BE CHALLENGED ALONG THE WAY.

Take a moment. Catch your breath. Let all this information sink deep into every fiber of your being. But don't sit on the sidelines too long. Make the commitment to become an Ally, and get to work. Remember there is a war going on even as you read these words. Some Black woman somewhere is being offended and oppressed by a White woman. It happens multiple times every second of the day, every day. **You have three choices: remain an Antagonist, continue to straddle the fence of Advocacy, or take the big leap into Allyship and never look back.** The feminist movement needs to be shaken up and rebuilt on truth. The voices of the movement need to be diverse and equally valued and heard. The women's empowerment movement is about to get a WAKE-UP call it will never forget. Too many women are being hurt by other women. Too many women are being left out, denied, devalued, and dismissed. Too many women in powerful positions are living a lie. Too many women leaders, coaches, service providers, mentors, and teachers are NOT walking their talk. The women's empowerment arena is sadly and dangerously participating in *Cliques, Catfights,* and *Colorblindness.* Women all over the planet are waiting for you and me to get our crap together so we can heal and save the world.

You've got a long journey ahead of you. There is no real blueprint. You'll have to fumble your way through this. You're going to make mistakes. You're going to get very overwhelmed, and you may even want to quit. **Welcome to the world of racial justice!** What you are about to experience comes nowhere close to what women of color and Black women experience daily, in too many ways to count, and at a rate and weight that you'll never know. **If we can carry the burden of the infliction of racism on our backs every day, surely you can stand up and speak up about it.** There is more for you to learn and unlearn. The work never ends until racism is eliminated. **Your racial justice journey doesn't end until you take your last breath.** Now roll up your sleeves and consciously and intentionally do YOUR work!

WAKE-UP CALL QUESTIONS

Have you determined whether you are an Antagonist, Advocate, or Ally?

_____

_____

_____

_____

_____

What do you need to do to transition from one role to the next?

_____

_____

_____

_____

_____

_____

_____

_____

Specifically, what work do you need to do?

_____

_____

_____

_____

_____

_____

_____

Who are you going to share this message and this book with next? Make a list and make sure they get the WAKE-UP call!

_____

_____

_____

_____

_____

_____

_____

_____

_____

_____

AFTERWORD

AFTERWORD

It's 2015 and there are still racial barriers between Black and White women on so many interpersonal levels. **Unfortunately, race still matters!** It matters so much that White and Black women often don't know how to relate to or engage with each other in ways that foster deep understanding and trust. These same complexities exist between all races and between women and men. However, in my experience, establishing true, deep, lifelong, and personal *relationships* with White women has been the most exhausting and challenging due to everything I've shared with you throughout this book. I am happy to say that despite the difficulties, I have found success in establishing some *friendships* with White women, yet they continue to be pretty superficial. As long as we stay away from "race talks," it's all good. My circle of White friends who are willing to engage in difficult conversations about racism is growing.

In my opinion, a friendship and a relationship are different. To me, *friendships* are casual, surface-level connections, while *relationships* are deeper and more meaningful. I'd love to have some **real** relationships with White women; however, it's just as important for me to preserve my emotional and spiritual energy for my purpose work. I'm most interested in being in relationships with White women who have been doing Ally work for a while, or with women who are committed to becoming an Ally; anyone else definitely creates more Racial Battle Fatigue for me. True relationships are about give and take. I'm open to having relationships with people who are willing to pour in as much as they expect to receive.

I'm confident I am not alone in finding these types of relationships challenging to create and sustain, as this issue has been the topic of discussion among many other Black women I know, and maybe White women feel the same way. I was curious to know whether White women had the same questions or concerns. A few years ago, I decided to survey fifty women I know—twenty-five Black and twenty-five White—with ten questions regarding relationships between Black and White women. Forty-three women responded and shared their insights into this complex situation. This survey is not scientific, yet it is interesting and important. A few themes emerged from the women's survey responses:

A sense of urgency. Both White and Black women feel a strong need to improve relationships between the two races even if they are unsure how to go about it. White women reported being understood more by Black women than Black women felt understood by White women. Specifically, Black women reported they felt White women either did not understand them at all or rarely, while White women reported that Black women understood them often or sometimes.

Race does matter. Similar words and phrases appeared throughout the women's comments (including fear, lack of trust, denial, frustration, racism, prejudice, privilege, lack of education, stereotypes, lack of understanding, defensiveness, avoidance, and failure to actively listen to each other). Black women reported race as an issue that creates barriers based on personal experiences. Black women felt White women just don't get it, to the point of getting defensive or minimizing a Black woman's race-related experiences. White women seemed to put less emphasis on race being a major factor in the quality of relationships between Black and White women.

Clouded vision. White women tend to be unaware of the experiences faced by many Black women, and while they know that differences exist and create barriers, they are unsure what to do about the situation. A few White women indicated they understand the significance of race and acknowledged it is an issue that needs to be openly discussed. Black women reported being tired and frustrated with trying to help White women understand their plight.

A need to be understood. Black women know there are racial barriers, experience them often, and can articulate what they are. They seek to be understood, heard, validated, and treated fairly and equally. Black women expressed a strong need for their race to be seen, considered, valued, and appreciated. White women reported a desire to be understood (and possibly forgiven) for not knowing that race matters.

Complexity of barriers. The barriers are complex and different for each woman. Generally, the women surveyed reported fear, poor communication, lack of interest, and prejudice/racism as the primary barriers to building authentic, trusting relationships with each other. Black women reported their desire for White women to become educated and to stop using "not knowing" as an excuse for not engaging with sensitivity.

Solutions for change. It appears that women are seeking opportunities to be heard, to understand each other, and to engage in dialogue that helps them find common ground. Specific solutions included workshops, social activities, dialogue sessions, long-term relationship-building, and opportunities to role-play each other's life experiences. Black women clearly and strongly stated the lack of desire to "educate" White women, while White women felt it would be helpful if Black women "educated" them on their racial struggles and what White women could do to help.

The results of this informal, unscientific survey indicate there are problems that need to be addressed so that both Black and White women feel heard, understood, and validated. Fear is a significant factor, as is the need for dialogue to be honest, compassionate, and ongoing. The issues of race, privilege, prejudice, and racism must be part of the conversation. Otherwise, Black and White women will continue to engage superficially or to not engage at all.

White women... there is so much more I could tell you, but if what I've shared throughout this book is *still* not enough, continue to do your own research and work. Reading, watching videos, and attending cultural diversity workshops is a start, but **I guarantee you, you will NOT become an Ally using only these methods.** You've got to get outside of your comfort zone and go into the communities you want to learn about without expecting them to educate you. **You've got to want to do this because it's the right thing to do, not because you are feeling guilty about the social and racial injustices that are happening in the world.** *Your heart has to ache for social change.* Your mind must become consumed with being active in the fight for justice and equality for all. Your soul must beg you to take action, get involved, and be the change you want to see in the world. Social and racial justice work must become part of your everyday life. This is not a temporary fix. You must wholeheartedly and unapologetically do your part until you take your last breath.

It still amazes me how many people appear to be sleeping through life. I don't mean sleeping only through their own lives, but to what is really going on in the world today. I think when it comes to a deep understanding of social disparities (social and racial injustices), many people are in a coma, and for some, hitting the snooze button is their way of denying what is happening. I believe most of us have a general understanding of the "ills" within our society, such as poverty, homelessness, abuse, addiction, war, and maybe even racism. Yet on a deep, intimate level, I believe many folks are in a coma of denial or "lack of knowing." Maya Angelou said, **"When you know better, you do better."** Sure, there are many things going on in the world I don't know about. However, I do "know" two main sources of the world's pain are sexism and racism. Just imagine if we no longer operated from these two "isms." Oh, how much more harmonious, peaceful, and loving the world would be if we didn't have the capacity to hate, discriminate, or abuse our power and privilege. We may never be able to make those "isms" go away completely, but we can all do better!

The real question to ask yourself is, *"Do I want to do better?"* By "doing better," I mean becoming more knowledgeable and "awakened" to what is happening socially in your city, community, workplace, neighborhood, and family. A second great question is, *"How socially conscious are you willing to become?"* Social consciousness is the consciousness shared within a society. It can also be defined as social awareness: to be aware of the problems faced by different societies and communities on a day-to-day basis, and to be conscious of society's difficulties and hardships.

What kind of hardships are women of color facing in your city? What kind of issues are women of color dealing with in your community? What barriers are women of color experiencing in your workplace? Do the women of color in your neighborhood feel welcomed, or are there any in your neighborhood? If you have women of color in your family, what is it like for them? These are just a few questions to get the social consciousness juices flowing, but there is greater, deeper personal work to be done to really become awakened to what's happening in the world.

You might be surprised at the number of times I've heard statements suggesting that people are in a social

consciousness coma. Here are a few of my favorites; note that they are examples of microaggressions, aka modern racism:

- *"You mean that kind of stuff (racism/discrimination) still happens today?"*
- *"I simply see people; I don't see differences."*
- *"I think that if you just treat people with dignity and respect, there's no need to pay attention to differences."*
- *"You know, I experience discrimination too; we all do."*

There are many more statements like these, but I'm hoping these few will help you see how good, well-intentioned people are asleep. Great relationships are built on understanding. Therefore, it's critical that you obtain the best understanding of what is going on with as many different groups of people as possible. **You have to seek the "knowing" so you can be informed and aware of what may be happening in the lives of people who do not look like you.** It's not enough to say, *"I don't know what's going on."* You have the opportunity every day to wake up and ask yourself, *"How can I become more socially conscious today?"* This is especially true if you work and live in a "diverse" community. Be careful if you are making statements similar to those listed above; they will be hurtful to your friends, colleagues, students, clients, and family members.

Choose to wake up today! Choose to learn about what is going on in the world and in your community. **Hitting snooze is a form of denial, and when you deny someone's experience, you support the oppressor and perpetuate oppression, intentionally or not.** Know that being silent on issues of race or discrimination is one way to agree with them. Each of us can take action every day to understand the disparities that others face and do something to help eliminate them. Being in a coma, hitting snooze, failing to know, and being afraid to take action only perpetuate the problem, and they are not justifiable excuses. Stop making excuses!

Wake up and be the difference in the world... your world, our world. THIS is your WAKE-UP call!

"When you know better, you do better."
—Maya Angelou

Class dismissed...

ABOUT THE AUTHOR

CATRICE M. JACKSON, MS, LMHP, LPC

Catrice M. Jackson is the Global Visionary Leader of the Awakened Conscious Shift, the CEO of Catriceology Enterprises, an international speaker, and a best-selling author. Catrice is passionate about empowering people and making an impact in the world. She's a humanist and activist dedicated to social and racial justice, because without either, people cannot fully or rightfully thrive in life. As an educator, consultant, and speaker, Catrice blends psychology, social consciousness, racial justice, and leadership wisdom into meaningful messages that propel people into action. Catrice is a dynamic difference maker with a voice that's unflinching, authentic, and powerful.

Catrice is the catalytic creator of SHETalks WETalk Race Talks for Women, and of WETalks for Women of Color. She is strong medicine and serves up the hard truths necessary to eliminate the lethal infection of racism from humanity. She realizes that her approach may be rebuked and her flavor undesired. Catrice knows she is not for everyone and that everyone won't like her, and she is unbothered by both. She is unmoved by naysayers and does her work authentically and unapologetically with a revolutionary spirt. She believes that justice is love.

For as long as I can remember, I've always had something to say. I'm often compelled to speak up for the underdog and about the injustices in the world. I have a passion for raising difficult topics and engaging in courageous conversations, conversations that challenge "the way things are" and help transform lives. I value truth, freedom, authenticity, courage, and peace, and I intentionally infuse my core values into every human engagement, keynote speech, training, and workshop, and on any platform for which I am called to be a voice.

Empowering the lives of people is my passion. I'm on a relentless mission to make a difference, to do work that is meaningful, and to inspire others to use their gifts for social change. I believe justice is love in action, and I'm committed to loving on humanity by being an activist for racial justice. I'm here to challenge the status quo, to disrupt injustice everywhere, to dismantle systems of oppression, and to wake people up into an awakened, conscious way of being, living, and engaging.

EDUCATION

- PhD, Organizational Psychology, Walden University (dissertation in progress).
- MS, Human Services/Counseling, Bellevue University. GPA 3.97.
- BS, Criminal Justice Administration, Bellevue University. GPA 4.00 (dean's list).
- Licensed Practical Nurse, Western Iowa Technical Community College.
- Certified Domestic Abuse and Sexual Assault Advocate, Trainer, and Speaker

RESOURCES FOR THE JOURNEY

YOUR HOMEWORK

I have read several great books that offer practical information on understanding racism and White Privilege, and that provide effective strategies on embracing and fostering diversity and inclusion. While I believe you must learn from personal experiences and people who are different from you for the best education, the resources listed in this section will give you fundamental information on how to expand on and apply what you've learned in Antagonists, Advocates, and Allies.

I also suggest you begin making personal connections with other White people who've committed to becoming anti-racist activists, who are already on the journey toward Allyship. At the end of the day, however, you cannot count on them or people of color to get you to your destination. You MUST be driven, passionate, and intentional while consciously pursuing your own path to becoming a racial justice Ally. This means you must take full responsibility for the consequences of your actions or lack thereof. This is YOUR journey and no one else's. Stay on the journey no matter how difficult it becomes; it does not end until you take your last breath. It's time to get to work!

BOOKS

Berger, Maurice. *White Lies: Race and the Myths of Whiteness.* Farrar, Straus and Giroux, 2000. Berger was one of just a few white kids in a New York City housing project in the 1960s. His father was a liberal White Jew who admired Martin Luther King Jr.; his mother was a dark-skinned Sephardic Jew who hated Black people. He describes his journey toward understanding race and racism.

Brodkin, Karen. *How Jews Became White Folks and What That Says About Race in America.* Rutgers University Press, 1998. Brodkin shows how Jewish immigrants assimilated within the framework of Whiteness and discusses "racial assignment" (sometimes Jews have been "assigned" to the White race; other times, they have been an "other"). Counters the "pulling yourself up by your bootstraps" myth.

Carter, Jessica Faye. *Double Outsiders: How Women of Color Can Succeed in Corporate America.* JIST Works, 2007. Carter provides a unique guide that not only helps women of color (of all shades) navigate corporate America, but also helps corporate America understand, recruit, and retain this critical and fast-growing employee demographic. Includes personal stories and key insights into these women's experiences, cultures, and achievements. Carter is African American.

Griffin, John Howard. *Black Like Me: 50th Anniversary Edition.* Wings Press, 2011. Griffin, a White man, darkened his skin and traveled through parts of the South as a Black man. He documented his experiences, first in an article published in Sepia magazine, then in this book (first published in 1961).

Guglielmo, Jennifer and Salvatore Salerno. *Are Italians White? How Race is Made in America.* Routledge, 2003. This collection of essays by Italian Americans describes their complex experiences with race, racism, and White Privilege.

Halsell, Grace. *Soul Sister: 30th Anniversary Edition.* Crossroads International Publishing, 1999. Like John Howard Griffin, Halsell (a White woman) darkened her skin and traveled through parts of the South as a Black woman. Soul Sister (first published in 1969) and Griffin's Black Like Me helped open White Americans' eyes to the realities of everyday racism.

hooks, bell. *killing rage: Ending Racism.* Holt Paperbacks, 1996. This collection of essays is written from a Black and feminist perspective and discusses topics including the anger felt by those who endure everyday racism, friendships between Black and White women, and psychological trauma among African Americans. hooks (née Gloria Jean Watkins) is African American.

Ignatiev, Noel. *How the Irish Became White.* Routledge, 1995. Ignatiev describes how the Irish immigrants to the U.S. in the 18th century "assimilated" in jobs, unions, and government by separating themselves from and excluding Blacks. Ignatiev is White.

Johnson, Allan G. *Privilege, Power, and Difference.* McGraw-Hill, 2005. Johnson describes how systems of privilege work (gender, race, ethnicity, sexual orientation, physical abilities, age, income, education, geographic) and discusses how to be part of the solution. Johnson is White.

Jones, Charisse and Kumea Shorter-Gooden. *Shifting: The Double Lives of Black Women in America*. Harper Perennial, 2004. Based on research from the African American Women's Voices Project, this book looks at how Black women in the U.S. "shift" between Black and White versions of themselves (including roles, language, internal thoughts, and more) to survive racism and other challenges. Jones and Shorter-Gooden are African American.

Kivel, Paul. *Uprooting Racism: How White People Can Work for Racial Justice*. New Society Publishers, 2002. Kivel describes the dynamics of racism in society, institutions, and daily life, and provides information on how White people can work for racial justice. Kivel is White.

Rothenberg, Paula. *Invisible Privilege: A Memoir About Race, Class, and Gender*. University Press of Kansas, 2000. Born into a wealthy and privileged White Jewish family, Rothenberg shares what she learned by studying her own privilege through the lenses of race, class, and gender.

Sue, Derald Wing. *Microaggressions in Everyday Life: Race, Gender, and Sexual Orientation*. Wiley, 2010. Sue describes the phenomenon of "microaggressions," the subtle-but-painful, often unintentional, slights and other biases that people inflict on one another, especially by the dominant culture onto members of marginalized groups. Sue is Asian American.

Ware, Vron. *Beyond the Pale: White Women, Racism, and History*. Verso, 2015. An important classic about the historical meanings of Whiteness, the historical roles of White women in racism, and the political relationships between Black and White women. Ware is White.

Wise, Tim. *Speaking Treason Fluently: Anti-Racist Reflections From an Angry White Male.* Soft Skull Press, 2008.

—. *Between Barack and a Hard Place: Racism and White Denial in the Age of Obama.* City Lights Publishers, 2009.

—. *White Like Me: Reflections on Race from a Privileged Son.* Soft Skull Press, 2011. Wise is a White man who speaks about Whiteness, White Privilege, and racism on U.S. campuses. He has written many articles and books on these topics, including the three books listed here.

Made in the USA
Middletown, DE
20 June 2020